The Million Dollar Total Business Transformation

By Walter Bergeron

The Million Dollar
Total Business Transformation

ISBN 978-1477401354

Special Sales

The Million Dollar Total Business Transformation book is available at special discounts for bulk purchases, sales promotions, special events, premiums and give-aways. For more information please visit:

www.walterbergeron.com

Free $997 Value

Audio Programs

Newsletters

Webinars

Online Resources

Go directly to:

www.walterbergeron.com

Acknowledgements

I do want to thank everyone that helped me accomplish this life changing goal starting with my wife of 19 years Jana Bergeron for having the confidence in me to let me take these risks and helping to make sure they paid off.

Lee Milteer for giving me opportunities I would have never had and the confidence to go for it.

Ron Penksa for pulling along me every step of the way, an amazing steak and truly inspiring conversations.

Linda Bergeron for the detailed editing and encouragement.

Carrie Lee and her husband Rollyn Lee for help with preparing for my presentation and for all the hugs during SuperConference.

Steve Wedeking for the words of encouragement and a beer to settle the nerves.

Aldon Hilton for the reference material and support.

Forrest Walden and Jim Cavale, Infusionsoft Ultimate Marketers of the Year, for encouraging me every step of the way.

Some new great friends for like Shaun Buck and Brodie Tyler, I want to see if we can meet up next time I am in Idaho visiting my wife's family.

I am sure I have missed many people and they all deserve my deepest Thank you.

Contents

Chapter One

"Planet Dan"
The Journey Begins

My journey to planet Dan began back in the early 90's, but I had no idea back then that I was going to land here. It was at that time I took the first steps towards implementation. While I was in the Navy, setting out to sea for weeks and then months at a time I would wander into bookstores prior to our voyage and find things to read that would give me some inspiration and not make those long lonely trips so unbearably boring. The self-help section was my usual choice and Tony Robbins tended to be my author of choice. The many books he wrote led to the tapes, then eventually CD's. Those CD's would be my constant companion on my long land trips. At the time I did a lot of driving to visit Jana, my girlfriend at the time and now my wife of 19 years. I had exactly 53 hours of time off in a row and I would spend 13 hours driving from San Francisco, California to Boise, Idaho then spend 27 hours with Jana and then another 13 hours of driving back to the Navy base. So with 26 hours of driving every 3 weeks, as well as lots of time at sea I was able to go through a lot of audio books.

That immersion in self-help and self-improvement continued through the years and I always had some book I was reading or CD in my truck I was listening to. The authors tended to be all in the same realm from Tony Robbins, to Jay Abraham, Michael Gerber and then eventually to Dan Kennedy.

I began my company called Power Control Services in 1996 after I served in the United States Navy for 6 years as a Nuclear Reactor Operator, and yes I do glow in the dark in case you were wondering. My experience in the Navy led to an "entrepreneurial seizure" and in a 400 square foot shed out in the middle of the sugar cane fields in Louisiana I started repairing industrial electronics for the local manufacturing plants. We perform component level repair to circuit boards, which means we replace the tiniest resistors and capacitors and miniscule transistors on high end, very expensive electronic automation equipment. Fast forward 15 years and now I have 2 repair centers, one in Broussard, Louisiana and the other in Atlanta, Georgia with over 40,000 square feet of building which makes us the largest national facility 100% dedicated to industrial electronic repairs. There are larger and there are higher volume facilities but they all do other things like sell new products and offer many other services, we focus only on repairs of electronic equipment. We also have 4 sales locations in Texas, Missouri, Nebraska and Georgia with outside sales staff manning those locations. We have had positive growth every year for the past 15 years and 2011 was our best year grossing $1.7 Million dollars in sales. We have a total staff of 15 employees with another 9 outside independent sales representatives.

In 2010 I read one of Dan's books, the "The Ultimate Marketing Plan". That led me to the free Gold Membership and more of his books. It was refreshing to read about this completely new topic, since E-myth and other business books focused on the production and operation side of the company and always seemed to steer clear or just lightly touch the marketing and sales aspects of my business. I dabbled in Dan's ideas, did a little work on my USP, wrote an email, I even joined Infusionsoft and it was a really pretty icon on my desktop. I never really implemented anything of significance and so I never really saw any results that were significant. You see

I wish at that point I could have had a conversation with Dan Kennedy because my business was different and Dan had no idea that what I was up against in my market was completely different and this stuff from other industries would never work in my business. YEAH RIGHT! Can you imagine if I would have had the audacity to get an audience with Dan at that point? Looking back at this now I wonder how I made any changes at all with such a terrible attitude and closed mind. Anyway, we do sell things in what I thought was a different manner, though I would later find out that Dan is quite an expert at my industry when I finally did get my one on one time with him in Cleveland at a Platinum Mastermind meeting, but we'll get to that later. You see Power Control Services sells business to business, actually that is not exactly correct. We sell our services to other businesses that sell our services to yet another business. So that makes us B2B2B. Our salesmen sell our repair services to other salesmen who in turn sell our repair services to maintenance personnel at manufacturing plants. An example of what this means would be like our good client Tyson Foods, Inc. Tyson takes live chickens and turns them into dinner. The way they do that is by using lots of equipment controlled by electronic automation. Meaning that most of the work is done by machines and these machines break down and that's where we come in. We fix the equipment that breaks down and they pay their vendor who in turn pays us. Oh what a tangled web we weave!

In September of 2011 I attended the FAST Implementation Boot Camp in Chicago with Bill Glazer. On September 20th at 3:31pm I experienced an epiphany. At that exact moment a light bulb went off in my head, the heavens opened up and the angels began to sing when in Bill Glazer's conclusion of the 2 day conference he said to look around at my peers. That out of the person to my left and the person to my right that at most only one of us would actually implement and take action and experience a significant change in his life from the priceless golden nuggets of information he was giving away to us. You see the last 2 days I got to know the person to my left and the person to my right. The guy to my left had a struggling furniture store and was being hurt by commoditization of his products and fierce competition. And the guy to my right was making a musical education product in his basement and needed to market it to get it off the ground. And when Bill said to look to my left, my furniture store friend was gone because he had more pressing issues with some fire he had to put out at the office. My friend to my right was SLEEEPING, he was actually snoring and missed the last 45 minutes of Bills presentation, not to mention countless other times he had dozed off. So my epiphany was that it was me who was going to implement, it was going to be me who was going to have a significant life impact by taking action on what I had just learned. And that is exactly what I did.

3 of the golden nuggets that I took away from that 2 days turned out to be priceless and what made all the difference in what I was able to accomplish over the next 90 calendar days.

1 – Take Massive Action Every Single Day

2 – Good Is Good Enough

3 – Simultaneous Implementation

1 – Take Massive Action Every Single Day

This was huge because I took an 11 x 17 sheet of paper and taped this to the wall near my desk so I would see it every single time I went into my office. I knew that if I continued to take "baby steps" then I would get "baby results" and that was simply unacceptable any longer. Massive action meant that I would also probably make massive mistakes and make a massive fool of myself – SO WHAT! I was the CEO, The President of the company and if it took me making huge errors and making myself look stupid then that was exactly what I was going to do and so that is exactly what I did.

I had to first get myself a work environment that allowed me the time and privacy I needed. So my first act of massive action was to put signs up on my office door and even along the walls to my office. **"GO AWAY", "YES I DO BITE", "IF THERE IS A FIRE – PUT IT OUT", "IF THERE IS AN EMERGENCY DIAL 911", "LEAVE ME ALONE"**

And hey, they worked. I was left undisturbed most of the time and my staff adjusted quickly by simply emailing me from the next office down the hall and I took care of things when I would take breaks.

After a few weeks my staff would start to ignore the signs, but I was just as determined to keep the work environment as productive as possible, so I had to take massive action again.

This may seem irrelevant but follow me on this. I was born on Halloween, yep October 31st, and so this holiday has always meant a great deal to me. I dress up in a costume every year, and yes even now I dress up and we throw a BIG Halloween/Birthday party. Over the years my wife has taken this to a whole new level. We now go shopping in August and start to prepare for the big party.

She has accumulated 10 pallets, yes 10 forklift sized pallets of Halloween decorations. 6 foot wide by 6 foot tall by 8 foot high pallets of every imaginable Halloween decoration including 8 life sized animated horror movie props. One of those animated props is Michael Meyers, of the famed Halloween movies. So back to my massive action.

Hockey mask on and knife in hand, I placed Michael Meyers just outside my office door with those signs taped all over him to "STAY AWAY", "OWNER BITES REALLY HARD" and wouldn't you know it, it worked again. Everyone left me alone so I could continue my trek into marketing implementation.

I also realized that 5 days a week was not enough, even during the weekends my mind would be racing with ideas and enthusiasm about the marketing ideas from the week. I would wake up on Saturday mornings with these thoughts, but by Monday they would be gone. So I took massive action again and started waking up an hour earlier than the rest of the household, sit at my laptop with a cup of "Joe" and I would write sales letters, and make revisions to copy and sometimes just THINK. In the peace of the early morning before the sun had come up I would just think and dream of what I am accomplishing and make it real in my mind, that the reality of success had already happened and I was living the life I imagined. And then I would get right back at it with an all new vigor.

So if you ever have an excuse that your staff won't leave you alone or you just can't find the time. You just need to dig a little deeper and find a more creative and totally extreme way to MAKE that time. MAKE it happen. MAKE it massive every single day.

2 – Good Is Good Enough

This part of my new philosophy is hard to swallow. I am an engineer by trade and for years and years, PERFECTION was good enough. Pursuit of perfection and only your best was good enough, were the mantra's I lived by. "If it ain't your best, then it ain't ready to send to your clients" that is what I pounded into my skull year after year. So this new philosophy of good is good enough is a real tough one to overcome.

Moving forward however, a new mantra sprung forth, and I decided that "The third time is a charm" would be my good is good enough measuring stick or mantra. I would work on something and give myself 3 revisions, then I would send it out the door to my clients. If I couldn't make it perfect after 3 tries, then so be it, errors and all were going out the door and I would just have to make corrections after the fact, when and if they ever were needed. This book is a perfect example of that. There are errors, there are things that could be worded better and more eloquently but after 3 tries, I am sending this to be published and I'll fix errors later but I am getting this thing out the door right away and not looking back wishing I had done a better job. A good book published is significantly better than a perfect book unpublished.

3 – Simultaneous Implementation

This part of my philosophy seems to defy physics, you can only do one thing at a time. You can only be in one place at a time and it is physically impossible to do anything other than one thing at a time. Well, that is in essence a correct assumption but what I wanted to do was to get a task completed up to a point that I could simply go no further. What that meant to me was for example…

When I started my newsletters.

I would do as much as I could as fast as I could and then I would hit a roadblock. Sometimes I would simply run out of ideas, sometimes my eyes would start to cross because I had been staring at the computer screen far too long or sometimes I just got bored with what I was doing. So I would then stop go take care of something in the office, or put stamps on envelopes or go fold some long form sales letters or some other task that would move me forward, onto something that gave me more satisfaction and that I could make more progress on. I would come back to the newsletters after a couple of hours and finish them up but at the end of the day I had two or three implemented strategies and that made multiple things happen at the same time. I did this every day and then as different projects took different timeframes to complete after a couple of weeks it was like every day something new was being completed and getting fully implemented. That fueled my enthusiasm so I worked even harder to make that happen again. I got a little drunk on accomplishment and I liked it, so I did it even more.

So I followed my 3 new found principles of implementation and for some reason I really felt that this was going to be a turning point in my life. I felt that landing on "Planet Dan" was profound enough of an event, that I wanted to make sure I documented what I did so that I would be able to share it with someone, anyone that might find it of value. I grabbed a single subject notebook and tied a pen to it so I never had an excuse why I didn't at least jot down what I had done, the thoughts in my head or the training I went through. I also thought that if I was going to truly make this happen that this was another method to make sure I did something every day so I wrote the date on every page and I was determined never to have a blank page in that notebook. Keep in mind that while doing this I also had the day to day tasks of a CEO within the same company I am transforming, no small task. Did I also mention that we had just purchased and renovated a 32,000 square foot building and moved the entire business just 30 days prior to all this? Yeah, we were pretty busy with other things on top of a major marketing effort.

What follows in the next pages is 90 calendar days, roughly 64 working days, of what I did every day including many weekends. The actions I took to implement my marketing plan and what I went through to accomplish the results I wanted. These actions were what it took to earn my business **$1,120,197.77** of true client value and earn me the title of "Marketer of the Year" simply by implementing a few of the many principles I learned when I landed on "Planet Dan".

I have many more examples and details of this at:
www.walterbergeron.com

Chapter Two

The First Month Is The Hardest

Day 1
9/21/11 - Wednesday

- I returned home from my trip to Chicago, from the GKIC FAST Implementation Boot Camp. Today will be the first day of not making any more excuses, taking things for face value and not over analyzing what needs to be done and just doing it. Man, all of this crap sounds so cliché and I can hear the words of all those motivational speakers in my head and it sounds so cheesy, so utterly embarrassing to say out loud. But, I don't care. This is the tipping point and I am going to do absolutely everything within my power to get as much done as I can, as quickly as possible.
- I took a look at our current vendor letter and applied some of the sales letter concepts – I put a deadline in it for responding, I put an offer in it and then I added a call to action with multiple ways to respond. I faxed the letter to our vendors in hopes of a better response to our open house event next month. Good is good enough.
- I tracked the responses from the open house efforts, GKIC says I need to know my numbers so I started a notebook to keep track of the numbers. Maybe I'll get more sophisticated but for now good is good enough.
- Call Ron Penksa with GKIC to see if he would give me some giveaways for our open house event, can't hurt to ask, but Ron said he would see what he could do. Something from a high level sales and marketing organization like Dan Kennedy would have tremendous value for our vendors and clients, because a lot of them are sales people. Not to mention it would give us a lot of credibility by giving them something like this. Massive action.

Day 2
9/22/11 – Thursday

- Got to work and sent out a revised second page to vendors to invite them to open house and this page had the response details, screwed up yesterday and forgot to send one of the ways to respond to the invitation. Ooops! Good is good enough kind of backfired today, so we made a correction and moved forward.
- Samson, the local rope manufacturing plant, just accepted our client invitation and gave me names of a few extra guys. This will help grow our list.
- Platinum Level Rebuild – swiped and deployed that name from GKIC, if it's good enough for them it's good enough for me. Sent some details on the preliminary offer of this program to Wayne Farms. This is helping me come up with a better USP though.
- Read on the internet ways to put together a newsletter. I found a guy named Jim Palmer and I ordered his book.
- Got started on USP first draft
- Jeff Wright, MAX mentoring coach wants me to list out my Strengths, Weaknesses, Opportunities and Threats.
- Thought about getting together a national program for ConAgra and Nestle, maybe Platinum parts will work here too.
- Brainstormed some ideas for the newsletter, I think a theme to each months' newsletter might be a way to grab clients' attention and help me get started instead of having a blank piece of paper every month.

Day 3
9/23/11 – Friday

- Ordered newsletter Guru book by Jim Palmer to help me figure out how to create a newsletter

- Completed the presentation in power point for ConAgra and Nestle, calling it Lifetime Warranty – This is what we might want to use for the Platinum program since it is probably the best warranty program we can offer and no one in our industry has anything even close. I will put all of the best services we offer into this package to make it unique and see if our competitors can keep up. It's time for us to be the leaders in this industry!

- Completed SWOT and sent it to Jeff Wright – Max mentoring coach.

  - **Strengths** - Fast, nimble little player in a big market.
  - **Weaknesses** - Small player with limited money for marketing and sales, we can't afford large campaigns to broad audiences, we can't afford to promote our brand, we need sales!
  - **Opportunities** - This direct marketing stuff is non-existent in our industrial market. Our clients are not going to know what hit them if we do this right.
  - **Threats** - Our competitors can copy what they see we have done, so making the marketing complex may help us out a lot.

- Completed our first USP – "Never pay for another Metal Detector repair again, ever!" Just change out the equipment type to fit the client's needs and we can quickly adapt it to multiple types of manufacturers to hit them with a very specific affinity.

Day 4

9/24/11 – Saturday

- Wrote down a ton of ideas for what to put into newsletter and the Jim Palmer book should be here in a few days to help me organize my ideas and figure out where to put them in the newsletter

- Completed marketing calendar for the 2012 year. Made a page for each month and really small font so I could fit everything into it. I know it is 99% wrong and these dates are really pretty useless but it gives me a perspective that I need to plan an entire year of campaigns and events ahead of time and 12 months isn't a whole lot of time to get everything done.

Day 5

9/26/11 – Monday

- Made phone calls to 15 vendors to make sure they got my invitations for the open house event. This also helped me develop a script to give to my customer service team so now they can do some of this for me, or at least they can use this and adapt it to the client phone calls. It's is really pretty ballsy of me to call my vendors and TELL them they need to participate to keep my business, 2 of them are so big they didn't care to lose me. So they lost me, to hell with them! Lots of vendors out there that will appreciate me more, I hope?

- Revised client open house invitation and faxed 108 faxes to clients using Infusionsoft. Got to do this efficiently and standing by the fax machine and dialing 108 numbers is not a good use of my time. Infusionsoft can do it for me for a few cents each, well worth the money.

- Holy Cow! I just got back 2 responses in 15 minutes from the faxes – Cool!! This is going into my bag of tricks, using lots of faxes instead of just emails, I guess since it's a physical copy it has a better response rate. Who'd of thunk it! Thanks Dan.

- Completed scrubbing active client list for incorrect fax numbers and names, etc… Man our list is way out of date, this is going to take forever. Get some coffee and get at it lazy bones, it's gotta' get done. Taking massive action was not easy today.

Day 6

9/27/11 - Tuesday

- Scheduled call with Jeff Wright – Max mentoring Coach. This guy has done a lot of stuff with his businesses and really an inspiration, he keeps telling me I am doing all the right things. I hope he's right.

- Began research on handling newsletter. Should it be a subscription? Do I send it to active clients only? What about inactive clients? Lots and lots of questions and I need to decide on those answers.
    - Some answers came today – My clients love pictures so heavy on the graphics and colors.
    - At first I am going to start with active clients and no subscription.

- Began research on Lost Customer Reactivation campaign. Bill Glazer has a pre-built campaign in the FAST Implementation Boot Camp binder – Swipe and Deploy baby!

- Did 1st rough draft on lost customer reactivation letter and rough draft on ideas for offers to lost clients. Made sure I included a deadline a call to action and with multiple ways to respond to the deal. Trying to make the deal pretty with lots of cool graphics. I am no graphic designer but it looks pretty good if I do say so myself.

- **ROADBLOCK – The guys installing some exterior signs just busted a gas line 15 feet from my office and we have to evacuate the entire building today – Thank you Fast Signs!! So I moved my car to a safe location and worked in my backseat with the air conditioner blasting – 87 degrees outside today.**

Day 7

9/28/11 – Wednesday

- Stayed at home for some alone time and undisturbed quietness to read the book I purchased, by Jim Palmer, a newsletter book. Got amazing ideas on how to move forward on the newsletter.

- I feel completely guilty for not going in to the office today. So I am telling myself that sitting out here by my pool, drinking some tea and reading a book is actually work and it is truly helping me implement my newsletter project. No one is going to believe you Walter – you are full of yourself! This is how you take massive action even when it defies conventional standard office wisdom.

- Began a list of what I want to put into newsletter and started collecting some of the materials, pictures and content ideas.

- My son's guinea pig is going to be a guest speaker in the newsletter – calling it Blaster's Corner – The pigs name is Blaster. This might be a lot of fun to do.

- **ROADBLOCK - My VP of Operations just stopped by my office to let me know the air conditioning system just stopped working and it is over 80 degrees in the production area. The technicians are sweating bullets and they can't work on energized equipment for fear of being electrocuted. Ah the life of a CEO, how do we keep production going now? The dollar store had 12 fans in stock so I bought those, we opened the windows and doors and relaxed the dress policy enough to get the guys producing repairs again.**

Day 8

9/29/11 – Thursday

- Worked on video for Platinum Rebuild Program using the Automated Webinar Cash Machine process and using powerpoint as the base for it. Thc Platinum Program is my way of putting our unique selling proposition into a membership program. It is a culmination of our best services including free shipping, lifetime warranty that NEVER runs out, priority repair head of the line privileges, 24/7 customer technical support with their own phone line and they know their technician by name.

- Well Walter, staying at home worked swimmingly "pardon the pun" because your work poolside just got the newsletter off the ground today. Couldn't do it for months and months before, but today it's coming to fruition. Took massive action and it payed off.

- Completed the video first rough draft using the AWCM template and ideas and techniques. Power point slides with me doing a voice over, my picture in the lower left-hand corner of each slide.

- Completed the webpage for the Platinum Program. I am no Joomla webpage expert so if it ever gets any more complicated than a few pictures and a little copy, gonna need some serious help.

- **ROADBLOCK - I just took a look at our monthly numbers and this is the second highest production month of the entire year. Everyone has been working tons of overtime to keep up, no wonder we are all exhausted.**

Day 9

9/30/11 – Friday

- Completed the second revision of the video for ConAgra Platinum program. This Platinum program might work for all our clients, but I want to test it out with these guys first and see if it has a big impact. All I have is a layout of the ideas, nothing for the actual production of this program has been set up. For now, all I am selling is an idea, a concept that is not developed or even thought through fully. Good is good enough and massive action.

- Scheduled a Go To Meeting webinar for next Wednesday to 80 companies that might be interested in the Platinum program – again, just selling an idea, this is going to bite me in the A*# I'll bet at some point down the road.

- Started 1st draft of newsletter on letter sized paper with only 2 pages. I may expand this later but for now this is all I think I can handle. Good is Good enough! Hey poolside work on Wednesday was effective.

Day 10

10/2/11 – Sunday

- Completed the second draft of the newsletter and let Jana (my wife of 19 years) look at it. This is the first marketing piece I have allowed her to look at and my tolerance for criticism is really small right now, go easy on me baby! She did go easy on me and helped me make a few corrections and then she helped me make it pretty and added colors. I made it all black and white and she added color to it, cool! So today, in order to take massive action, I had to call in some help.
- Jana took lots of Halloween decorations to work, I took Michael Myers for myself and put him near my office door. I've got plans for this guy.

Day 11

10/3/11 – Monday

- Completed 2nd draft of Lost Customer Reactivation campaign and I added a few copy doodles of my own. It will be Halloween so I put some ghosts and bats in the letter, a little outrageousness, hope the clients appreciate it.

- Did invitations to webinar for ConAgra and Nestle Platinum and did some webinar training with Go To Webinar website guys. My knowledge wasn't even good for the good is good enough philosophy so I got some help today.

- Had 2 of our customer service personnel, Pam and Tammy, make calls to all local clients about open house and document attendance responses. They used some of my script from the vendor calls, adapted it to their own needs and I made them document the script so I could use it for our next event. This will be how I took simultaneous action today to be able to re-purpose one developed system into more.

- **ROADBLOCK – Having a typical lunch day at the office by eating at my desk, except for the fact that I just spilled my entire drink onto my keyboard and now it won't work. Ran to office supply store and now I own a new fancy whizbang keyboard.**

Day 12

10/4/11 – Tuesday

- Call with Jeff Wright Max Mentoring Coach. He continues to tell me I am ahead of the game and implementing more than he expects and that I am doing the right things. I hope he's right or this is going to be a huge waste of resources.

- Completed Module 6 of Max mentoring program – this was a massive action today, that module is quite large.

- Trained on webinar hosting for tomorrows' webinar and did a trial run to make sure I don't screw it up. It's going to be a really high profile list of attendees so "Go big or go home" I might just wind up hitting this out of the park – Positive thinking can't hurt, right? Yep, Good is good enough.

- **ROADBLOCK - Sick little boy at work today. Stayed on couch near my office and watched TV most of the day while he ran a fever. I struggled to concentrate on work with the TV noise in the background. Just had to grin and bear it with my office door closed.**

Day 13

10/5/11 – Wednesday

- Worked on printing envelopes for newsletter, I am an MS Word delinquent. How do you add the stupid names from excel and get word to do the work for you!

- Worked on more content for October newsletter, I need to stay ahead of this so I can get everything printed and ready to send them out. I will also need to get way ahead of this for the next one if I plan to send it out by November 1st if possible.

- Put on first webinar without a hitch- YAAAYYY!! Almost 40 people attended and I got the questions answered live on the phone.

- Added quite a few questions and answers to presentation and prepared for second webinar today.

- Got a call from Ken with GKIC to see how service with Max mentoring is going and overall feeling with GKIC. I love you guys, can we get a man hug at some point Ken?

- Put on second webinar and it went great as well. All 80 of the invitees attended so this was pretty successful. I just don't know what I am going to do if they actually want to sign up for this Platinum program idea I am pitching to them.

Day 14

10/6/11 – Thursday

- Last few ideas went into newsletter – ALMOST DONE!! YEAH!

- Holy crap! They want to enroll into the Platinum program. I made Platinum Level Rebuild Program enrollment form, I put the horse before the cart again, got people interested and wanting the service and have no idea of how to enroll them, but I quickly got it done. Lots of incentive to get it done when someone is waiting for it.

- Entered new contacts into Infusionsoft from Webinar – I need to find an easier way to link Go To Webinar info into Infusionsoft, this is very slow to get done and I just want to move on. Suck it up and do it Walter! Back to the coffee pot, a few encouraging words from my wife, 5 minutes looking at a picture of my family and reliving a vacation we took to Florida last year to remember why this is worth it.

- **ROADBLOCK – Copier sales guys, excuse me "Digital Document Center" guys wanted to talk for hours about the new copier they just dropped off, Sorry guys I need to get stuff done so I had to excuse myself and tell them to leave and that I would call if I need them. I'm paying you so I need you to fit this into my schedule.**

Day 15

10/7/11 – Friday

- Completed newsletters, now fighting the $@%*'ng copier to print the envelopes – 1 at a time is ridiculous, this copier is a piece of %$#@!!!!!

- I figured out an easier way to do this, copier not so bad – just the copier operator needs a little training and a lot more patience. I want patience and I want it NOW! I had to call in re-enforcements from my copier tech team to settle my nerves and then walk me through the basics of how this copy machine works. Oh, by the way, copier guys get offended when you call it a copier these days. It's a "Digital Document Center" – whatever you say copier guy, thanks for all the help though!

- Cleaned up end user list more and ready to send out newsletters. Again, my list is so inaccurate and so many errors like no zip code, their first and last name is duplicated and on and on. This is massively frustrating and time consuming.

Day 16

10/8/11 – Saturday

- Printed all the newsletters and got them ready to mail, have 500 of them to send out to distributors and end users.

- My Dad happened to stop by the office this morning. We chatted about this marketing stuff, I am pretty sure he doesn't really get it. I don't know that I even get it. He helped me fold all those pages and pages of newsletters. Great to have him here helping me get these ready but explaining to him WHY I was sending these out was tough when I don't even know if this is going to work. He had a lot of questions and really so do I, but for now I'm going on blind faith that this is going to have some type of impact and make a difference, but I really don't know for sure.

- I need to get stamps and then get these into the mail on Monday. Does the post office deliver stamps?

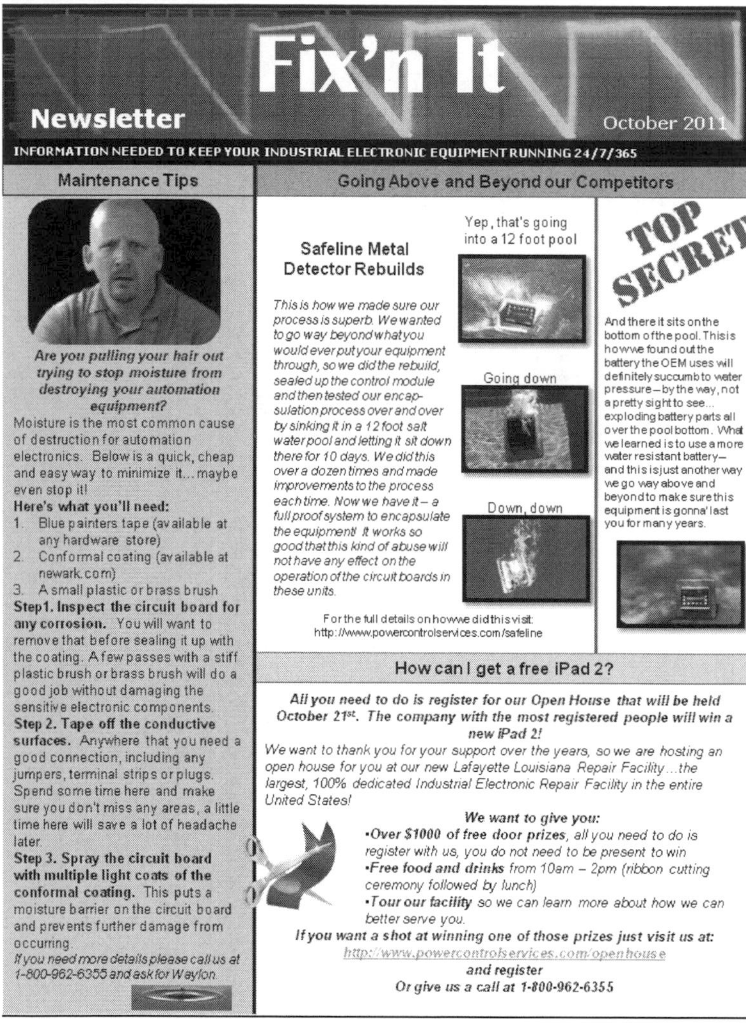

Fix'n It

Newsletter October 2011

INFORMATION NEEDED TO KEEP YOUR INDUSTRIAL ELECTRONIC EQUIPMENT RUNNING 24/7/365

Maintenance Tips

Are you pulling your hair out trying to stop moisture from destroying your automation equipment?

Moisture is the most common cause of destruction for automation electronics. Below is a quick, cheap and easy way to minimize it... maybe even stop it!

Here's what you'll need:

1. Blue painters tape (available at any hardware store)
2. Conformal coating (available at newark.com)
3. A small plastic or brass brush

Step1. Inspect the circuit board for any corrosion. You will want to remove that before sealing it up with the coating. A few passes with a stiff plastic brush or brass brush will do a good job without damaging the sensitive electronic components.

Step 2. Tape off the conductive surfaces. Anywhere that you need a good connection, including any jumpers, terminal strips or plugs. Spend some time here and make sure you don't miss any areas, a little time here will save a lot of headache later.

Step 3. Spray the circuit board with multiple light coats of the conformal coating. This puts a moisture barrier on the circuit board and prevents further damage from occurring.

If you need more details please call us at 1-800-962-6355 and ask for Waylon.

Going Above and Beyond our Competitors

Safeline Metal Detector Rebuilds

This is how we made sure our process is superb. We wanted to go way beyond what you would ever put your equipment through, so we did the rebuild, sealed up the control module and then tested our encapsulation process over and over by sinking it in a 12 foot salt water pool and letting it sit down there for 10 days. We did this over a dozen times and made improvements to the process each time. Now we have it – a full proof system to encapsulate the equipment! It works so good that this kind of abuse will not have any effect on the operation of the circuit boards in these units.

Yep, that's going into a 12 foot pool

Going down

Down, down

For the full details on how we did this visit: http://www.powercontrolservices.com/safeline

TOP SECRET

And there it sits on the bottom of the pool. This is how we found out the battery the OEM uses will definitely succumb to water pressure – by the way, not a pretty sight to see... exploding battery parts all over the pool bottom. What we learned is to use a more water resistant battery – and this is just another way we go way above and beyond to make sure this equipment is gonna' last you for many years.

How can I get a free iPad 2?

All you need to do is register for our Open House that will be held October 21st. The company with the most registered people will win a new iPad 2!

We want to thank you for your support over the years, so we are hosting an open house for you at our new Lafayette Louisiana Repair Facility... the largest, 100% dedicated Industrial Electronic Repair Facility in the entire United States!

We want to give you:

- ***Over $1000 of free door prizes**, all you need to do is register with us, you do not need to be present to win*
- ***Free food and drinks** from 10am – 2pm (ribbon cutting ceremony followed by lunch)*
- ***Tour our facility** so we can learn more about how we can better serve you.*

If you want a shot at winning one of those prizes just visit us at:

http://www.powercontrolservices.com/openhouse

and register

Or give us a call at 1-800-962-6355

I have many more examples and details of this at: www.walterbergeron.com

What they're saying about us

Thank you very much. I have recommended your company to a few other Maintenance Managers that I deal with I hope they do business with you. Your response to our needs have been great and look forward to doing business with you in the future.
David W Dunican
Maintenance Manager

Most importantly, the quality of the performance repairs has enhanced our reputation within this area and we have been able to improve our customer's operational efficiencies accordingly.
Chris A. Hyche
General Manager

Now this is a serious deal

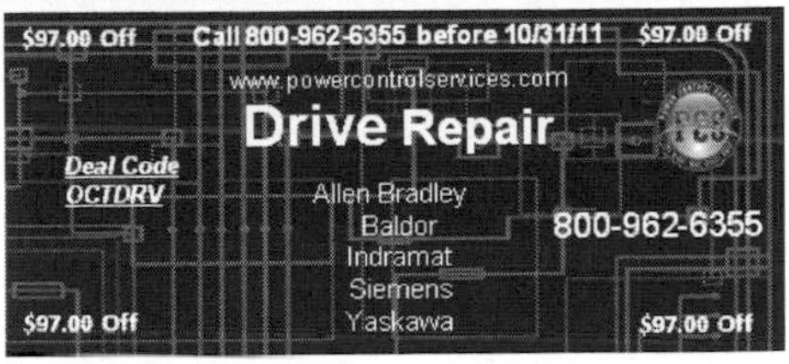

$97.00 Off
Call 800-962-6355 before 10/31/11
$97.00 Off
www.powercontrolservices.com
Drive Repair
Deal Code
OCTDRV
Allen Bradley
Baldor
Indramat
Siemens
Yaskawa
800-962-6355
$97.00 Off
$97.00 Off

Call right away for an RMA (return material authorization) have this coupon and the equipment part number handy and we'll get your $97.00 off price. If you call before 10/31/11 you will also receive free shipping as well as free priority service upgrade.

Happy Halloween Everyone!

You probably don't know this but Halloween is the President of our company's birthday and as you might expect he is a huge fan of all things haunted and ghoully. Over the years he has collected many ~~anima... animetron... enematronic~~ life sized figures and he stores them in one of our warehouses. So this year we decided to bring them out and place them around the office to officially kick off the Halloween season.

Headless Maiden and Lead Technician Chris Faulk. They scare clients as they come by the service counter

The Twins
Brandon Milam
And
The Mummy

We repair and test hundreds of food grade Safeline metal detectors every year and so we have a pretty extensive capability to scan food materials for any metal contaminates.

So this year we are going to scan all of our kids candy just as any overprotective parent would do.

What parent wouldn't take their kids candy from them and not let them eat it until they run it through an industrial, food grade ,conveyor fed metal detector? Seems perfectly reasonable to me.

Just clowning around

An idiot decides to start up a chicken farm, so he buys a hundred chickens to get up and running.
A month later he returns to the dealer to get another hundred chickens because the first lot had died.
Another month passes and he's back at the dealers for another hundred chickens, "I think I know where I'm going wrong" he tells the dealer,
"I think I'm planting them too deep."

A Little Office Humor
Once I came upon this pretty new temp standing in front of the paper shredder with a confused look on her face. I asked if she needed any help and she said, "Yeah, how does this thing work ?" I took the papers from her hand and demonstrated how to work the shredder. She stood there a moment with yet another confused expression, so I said, "Any questions?" She said, "Yeah, exactly where do the copies come out from ?

I have many more examples and details of this at:
www.walterbergeron.com

Day 17

10/10/11 – Monday

- Cleaned up Infusionsoft Lost Customer Reactivation Program list. I really hate these lists, I have done this with multiple lists and I hope this torturous activity ends sometime soon! Thank you mister coffee maker and "Hazelnut Blend" flavored coffee, a little treat for my efforts here. Massive action wasn't all that today.

- Sent out 11 Platinum level rebuild campaign enrollments. Now I have step 2 of 20 for this Platinum program done. Hopefully by the time I get 1 client enrolled I'll actually have a service to give them.

- Hey, the post office will actually deliver stamps to you, I just need to fax over the order form by 8 and they'll bring me stamps the same day. Man these guys are great!

- **ROADBLOCK – Clients are walking in all day long and I am so very thankful the signs we put up are effective BUT I need to keep moving forward. So I grabbed 2 of my customer service personnel and had them handle the clients when they walked in, I just showed them what I do and made them document it for future training.**

Day 18

10/11/11 – Tuesday

- Coaching call with Jeff Wright, still ahead of the curve, making his job of kicking me in the tail every week very easy. Maybe I should ask for a partial refund since I'm doing all the work? The truth is that knowing he is going to call me every single week and demand I tell him what I have gotten done drives me even harder to get more done than what he expects out of me. Massive action made easy with a swift kick in the "you know where"

- Sent out 500 newsletters to distributors and end users

- Received 2 Platinum enrollments back. I hope these guys are worth what I think they are worth, I looked at the Max mentoring training and I think I need to do another round of detailed market research to see what these clients are worth to me. It seems to be a lot of time spent with all the process to get these guys and they may not be worth it.

- Sent out 9 more Platinum enrollment forms, customized names and details for each client – way slow to do this and not sure if they are worth it.

- Planning on implementation package for service centers. I want to increase the value of these clients for the Platinum program so I need them to have their own customized marketing materials as well as detailed instructions on how to use them and when to use them.

Day 19

10/12/11 – Wednesday

- Sent out 16 more Platinum Level Rebuild Program enrollment campaigns

- Prepared Applied generic presentation for Jackson, Tennessee Area for National Account manager

- Designed 2 more pieces of marketing material for Platinum Level Rebuild implementation package. I am making progress but I also want to be able to continue this program without the same old way of sending out a salesman to the client for a face to face meeting. Need a secret weapon that works better than the face to face sales call same way that everyone else is doing it.

- Massive action was pretty easy today, good is good enough helped get those pieces out today and that enabled me to simultaneously implement on a whole new level.

Day 20

10/13/11 – Thursday

- Completed enrollment forms for all webinar attendees, now it is time to push the issue and get as many of these guys on board.

- I did a lot more research on this and these distributors are worth $34,575.98 each!!! Each one of them! So yes, the work that is going into this Platinum program is worth so much more than I originally thought.

- Completed Platinum Level Rebuild Program package components CD Case, CD, Instruction laminated handout. How could I put the video in a different format?

- Received 2 more enrollments from Service Centers – we now have 5 of them

- Updated presentation for platinum program to present in front of regional manager for largest client

- Received 3D Mail pieces from Travis Lee for our Lost Client Reactivation Campaign, he even sent a CD with the copy already done for me. So I took a lot of time with my first couple of drafts, I think this CD just made all that work useless. My good is good enough didn't come close to what Travis gave me for FREE. I need to figure out better ways to have others help me get more done with the valuable little time I have but money does not grow on trees, or does it?

Day 21

10/14/11 – Friday

- Sent out 6 Platinum Level Rebuild Program Packages, wow these are catching on quite well
- 4 Clients are complaining that they can't watch the webinar because the company doesn't allow internet access at work, they have to go home to watch it.
- Emailed all Platinum Level Rebuild Program clients another enrollment form and letter
- Got envelopes for boomerangs and found out that they won't fit – The instructions said I need #12 envelopes but I thought I could fit them in # 10, I was wrong – no way they fit into #10 envelope. Back to the office supply store to find out they are a special order item. Back to the office, 45 minutes online and now I have those pesky #12's on the way – be here Monday I think.

Day 22

10/17/11 – Monday

- I made a detailed list of preparations we need to make for the open house event. The event is this Friday and we have a lot of work to do. Think Good is Good Enough if for no other reason than you don't have much time.

- I sent out candy jars and gift cards to 2 clients that sent us feedback that we can use in our newsletters as well as we will put it into the marketing pieces we give away at the open house. Simultaneous implementation again.

- **ROADBLOCK – Staff came to me with a problem regarding our KPI's (Key Performance Indicators) They want a way to measure timeframes on many of these numbers and relate that to customer satisfaction surveys they had conducted. Solution was to take a working lunch in the conference room, I had them order pizza and we all got into the problem. We didn't get it all worked out, but enough of it was done that I didn't need to be involved any further.**

Day 23

10/18/11 – Tuesday

- I printed up the Lost Client Reactivation Program first letters and then folded them up to get them ready to mail

- Cleaned up list of lost clients in Infusionsoft so I could be ready to print up the envelopes. This is such a pain, I really despise cleaning lists. Needed some motivation so I took 5 minutes reflecting on that Florida vacation picture of my 8 year old little boy and my wife in her swimsuit didn't hurt either.

- I prepared the time table for Friday's open house event and got with everyone at the office so everyone knows what they are going to do. Ideally we would still like to have the production team unaffected by this event but I also want them to play a role and take ownership of the outcome. It'll also give them a great opportunity to meet the people they are servicing the equipment for.

- Sent out 4 Platinum Level Rebuild Packages. These are newly enrolled clients and now I made them a done for you marketing system to use to sell our service to their clients. A done-for-you system of pre-made marketing pieces so it makes their jobs easier to sell our services. Genius Walter! But swiped and deployed from GKIC of course.

Day 24

10/19/11 – Wednesday

- Conference call with Jeff Wright Max Mentoring Coach. Jeff had some great advice about our event on Friday. We need to capture as much contact information as we can from attendees. People are going to show up that we don't know and we need to make the most of that to grow our list. So when we give things away, have them sign for it, so we can announce their name and send them a Thank you card as well as use this primarily to market to them, since this is our primary goal.

- Sent out 5 Platinum Level Rebuild Program packages, oh man this is starting to take off quite a bit.

- Making preparations for open house on Friday. The tent will arrive in the morning as well as chairs and tables. We walked and marked the site for placement of everything. The entire Louisiana team got involved and it was great to see everyone excited about the day.

Day 25

10/20/11 – Thursday

- Lots of preparation for open house. I am really nervous about no one showing up and I have all these vendors here expecting me to provide them some value for what they paid for. The marketing was there but it wasn't very good stuff and response was OK but not great.

- Man I'm giving away an Ipad – That should draw people in plus free food. Vendors also said they invited some of their clients for us. It is truly wonderful to have vendors that not only support you, but pay to be at your event and then invite their clients to experience your open house. These are my vendors for life. What a great way to build a relationship with another company that supports us. Massive action today for sure.

Day 26

10/21/11 – Friday

- Open house event from 10 to 2, everyone came in an extra hour early to help make final preparations

- About 50 clients showed up and I think all the vendors made some sales. I gave the vendors a list of everyone that attended, a glowing letter of recommendation as well as personal letters I sent out to my clients on behalf of the vendors. I hope they get some more work because I plan on asking them to sponsor the event again in a few months. Simultaneous implementation.

- Mailed out 100 letters to Lost Clients, Evan (my 8 year old son) was out of school today for teacher in service, so he helped me do it. What a little trooper, he sat there patiently and folded letter and then sealed them for me and put on the stamp. Not bad when you consider he would much rather play his video games or just watch T.V., especially because now Dad is starting to become very uncool at this age.

Chapter Three

Things Are Starting To Fall Into Place

This is the start of the second month of full on implementation. The first month was pure struggle and I had to find motivation every single day to make these things, these actions of marketing, a habit that I would be able to use to keep the momentum going.

I used any ounce of creativity I could find within myself to help build the materials I implemented. I used every resource I could think of that was free or that I could call in favors to use. I had a sickness in my stomach every time I would send something out to a client. I was so very afraid that someone was going to call me and be furious that I said something offensive or that they hated what I was sending to them and they were going to tell everyone they knew just how much of an idiot I was for attempting to use this type of marketing in this industry. Well that call never came. I never got a complaint, in fact, it was just the opposite. People started to make comments that what they saw from us was unique and they were really happy that someone was paying attention to them finally. This was very encouraging and so I kept going. During the next month I gained more momentum and things began to progress even faster. The time for being timid and apprehensive was over and I launched a full on assault on our marketing system. I really got it moving and built it even faster during month 2.

Day 27

10/24/11 – Monday

- Sent out all 266 Lost Client Reactivation letters. Sounds easy. Printed, folded stuffed and stamped 266 individual pieces of mail. Not fun but got it done.

- Completed 60% of November newsletter. Getting a real head start for next month so it's not the middle of the month before our clients get it this time. I would like to send it the first day or so of the month if I can.

Day 28

10/25/11 – Tuesday

- Worked on more of November newsletter content, this is going slightly faster than last month but still a very time consuming process that requires a lot of thought and creativity. I am considering outsourcing this, but I don't want some canned run of the mill newsletter. I don't want it to be boring and look like everyone else's mundane crap!

- I held training with my customer service reps on the new deals we are now offering, how to change the sales process and how to answer phones to get referrals more easily as well as to solicit testimonials with every call.

- Completed 1st draft of long form handwritten sales letter. I found a way to put my handwriting into a font that I can import and use in all my projects. So now these letters really will be in my own handwriting.

Day 29

10/26/11 – Wednesday

- I completed the 2nd revision of long form handwritten sales letter. I added a few copy doodles on my own as well as some color pictures and it also helped me develop a triple guarantee to help my clients feel more at ease with our services.

- Coaching call with Jeff Wright, a few bright ideas on what to do with the aftermath of a very successful open house. How to capitalize on these new found relationships and make the most of the event.

- More ideas from Jana on November newsletter, she has a really keen eye on making it colorful and much more interesting to read. She always adds some shapes and different fonts to it. I am improving but she really makes it sparkle with her finishing touches. She is a valuable resource for me and she is starting to take massive action for me.

- Ron Penksa called and asked if I would do a phone interview with him on Friday. How very flattering and that gives me an idea. Why don't I do the same thing with our clients? Why don't I ask them to do a "Success Interview" over the phone? It'll give me a great bond with them as well as an extended testimonial that I can use in an audio CD to send out with our newsletters, just like the GKIC monthly gold CD. I can also get it transcribed and use quotes out of it for written testimonials. If I ask for a picture as well I can make those testimonials even more powerful. Man I think I'm onto something here. Simultaneous implementation.

Day 30

10/27/11 – Thursday

- I completed final revision of Platinum Level Rebuild Program to send to General Managers and Account managers in a nice concise written format

- Cleaned list for Platinum Level Rebuild Program – all day long, man this is so very time consuming and boring, but it has to be done – NO ROADBLOCKS are going to stop me from getting this done. So big gulps of coffee, a few minutes of visualizing being done and the sense of accomplishment and away I go! Massive action!

Day 31

10/28/11 – Friday

- Interview with Ron Penksa of GKIC. He had a great format for the interview and I am going to swipe and deploy that for my own interviews of our clients. I wonder if our sales clients will actually listen to testimonials. I guess they would if it was from another salesman. So I can do 2 different types of interviews. 1 with successful sales clients and 1 with successful maintenance clients, each would have a different target audience and I could put them with the newsletter I send out monthly. I could call it automobile university, probably stolen name from someone, and they could listen to it in their car on the way to work. Again Walter, Genius – and again, swipe and deploy from GKIC.

- Mailed out 68 long form letters to General Managers about Mailed out 66 long form letters to Account Managers about Platinum Level Rebuild Program

- **ROADBLOCK – Jana had major stress meltdown about Halloween party being just a couple of days away. Do I really need to address this now! Yes, I need to get her problems solved and stress reduced so she can help me get more things implemented. Called in staffing service help as well as employees kids to come and do decorating and clean up.**

Day 32

10/31/11 – Monday

- Worked on final content for November newsletter, just about to the good is good enough stage of this project.

- Worked on script for walk in clients, this location is prime walk in area and we are getting all sorts of people wondering what we do here. Maybe we need to get some signs up near the road and not just on the building.

- Birthday – Just turned 41 and feeling every day of that age. I am going to take my little boy "Trick or Treating" and then of course add the "Dad Tax" to his candy treasure. Yep, Dad gets ALL the peanut butter cups and kit kats. If you want me to dress up and take you then it's gonna cost you a few treats my young son. Actually I love getting dressed up like Frankenstein with the makeup and all and then scaring the little kids but I won't tell him how much fun I'm having since I am officially too old to ask for candy.

day

- Completed November newsletter and getting faster at this. At least twice as fast as the last time I did it.

- Completed rough draft of client walk in process

- With so many clients walking through the door I need to put up some exterior signs. So I worked on exterior sign layout with the help of magnetic marketing "Signs" book that I got as a bonus for the system. I am not going to put any of the standard contact information on these signs. Instead I am going to answer the most common questions I get when people walk in the door. "What do you guys do here?" *"The oldest equipment to the newest technology"* "How long does it take to get it done?" *"Drop it off today and pick it up tomorrow."* So I am going to continue this theme with the signs near the highway that would give us the largest impact for our money.

Day 34

11/2/11 – Wednesday

- Sent out November newsletter. I want to get a folding machine, my hands are raw from folding and stuffing all those newsletters. I went to an 11 x 17 format and now I need to fold each newsletter by hand 3 times so it will fit into an envelope. Looking on ebay today for something to make this easier.

- Coaching call with Jeff Wright. Jeff noted that one thing that is slowing down my progress is that I am doing everything myself. I would get more done much faster if I could delegate some of these tasks to others and then I could start to work on something new. I am getting lots done but I could multiply my efforts if I was able to use others to help. This may be in the form of current employees or outsourcing to staffing services or vendors that could do it better and faster.

- Customer service rep meeting about new monthly deals, walk in procedures and customer service kiosk area

- Sent out 2 more Platinum Level Rebuild Packages to enrollees

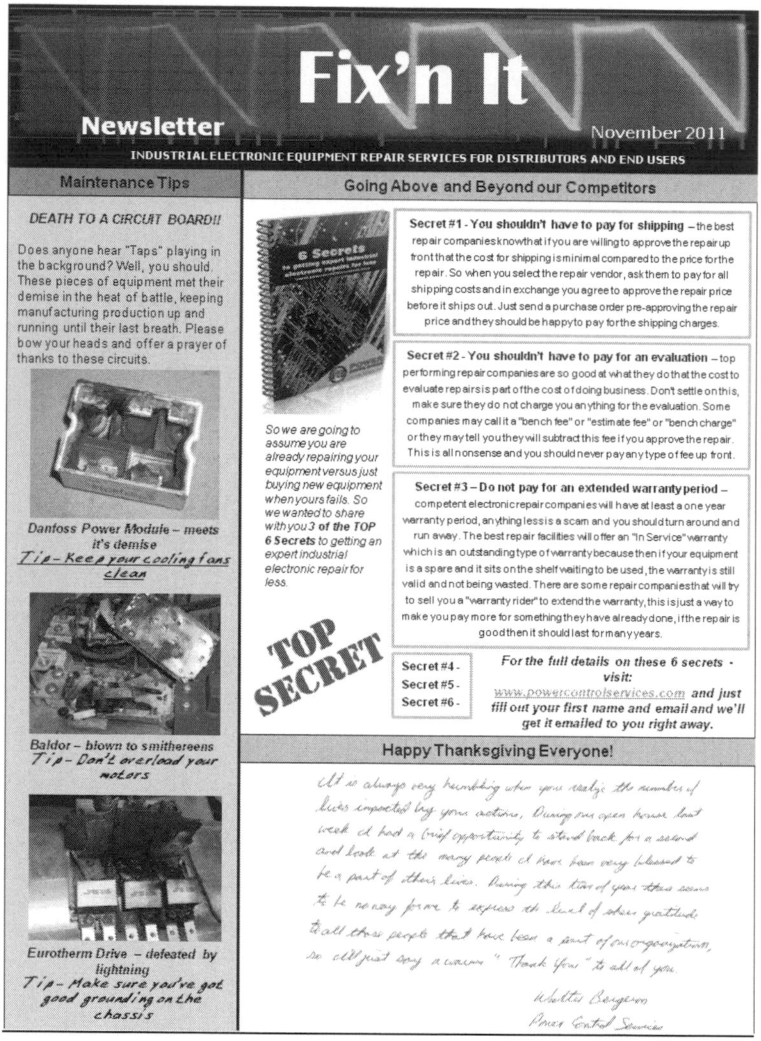

Fix'n It

Newsletter

November 2011

INDUSTRIAL ELECTRONIC EQUIPMENT REPAIR SERVICES FOR DISTRIBUTORS AND END USERS

Maintenance Tips

DEATH TO A CIRCUIT BOARD!!

Does anyone hear "Taps" playing in the background? Well, you should. These pieces of equipment met their demise in the heat of battle, keeping manufacturing production up and running until their last breath. Please bow your heads and offer a prayer of thanks to these circuits.

Danfoss Power Module – meets it's demise

Tip – Keep your cooling fans clean

Baldor – blown to smithereens

Tip – Don't overload your motors

Eurotherm Drive – defeated by lightning

Tip – Make sure you've got good grounding on the chassis

Going Above and Beyond our Competitors

6 Secrets to getting expert industrial electronic repairs for less

So we are going to assume you are already repairing your equipment versus just buying new equipment when yours fails. So we wanted to share with you 3 of the ***TOP 6 Secrets*** *to getting an expert industrial electronic repair for less.*

TOP SECRET

Secret #1 - You shouldn't have to pay for shipping – the best repair companies know that if you are willing to approve the repair up front that the cost for shipping is minimal compared to the price for the repair. So when you select the repair vendor, ask them to pay for all shipping costs and in exchange you agree to approve the repair price before it ships out. Just send a purchase order pre-approving the repair price and they should be happy to pay for the shipping charges.

Secret #2 - You shouldn't have to pay for an evaluation – top performing repair companies are so good at what they do that the cost to evaluate repairs is part of the cost of doing business. Dont settle on this, make sure they do not charge you anything for the evaluation. Some companies may call it a "bench fee" or "estimate fee" or "bench charge" or they may tell you they will subtract this fee if you approve the repair. This is all nonsense and you should never pay any type of fee up front.

Secret #3 – Do not pay for an extended warranty period – competent electronic repair companies will have at least a one year warranty period, anything less is a scam and you should turn around and run away. The best repair facilities will offer an "In Service" warranty which is an outstanding type of warranty because then if your equipment is a spare and it sits on the shelf waiting to be used, the warranty is still valid and not being wasted. There are some repair companies that will try to sell you a "warranty rider" to extend the warranty, this is just a way to make you pay more for something they have already done, if the repair is good then it should last for many years.

Secret #4 -
Secret #5 -
Secret #6 -

For the full details on these 6 secrets - visit: www.powercontrolservices.com and just fill out your first name and email and we'll get it emailed to you right away.

Happy Thanksgiving Everyone!

It is always very humbling when you realize the number of lives impacted by your actions. During our open house last week I had a brief opportunity to stand back for a second and look at the many people I have been very blessed to be a part of their lives. During this time of year there seems to be no way for me to express the level of sheer gratitude to all those people that have been a part of our organization, so I'll just say a warm "Thank You" to all of you.

Walter Bergeron
Power Control Services

I have many more examples and details of this at:
www.walterbergeron.com

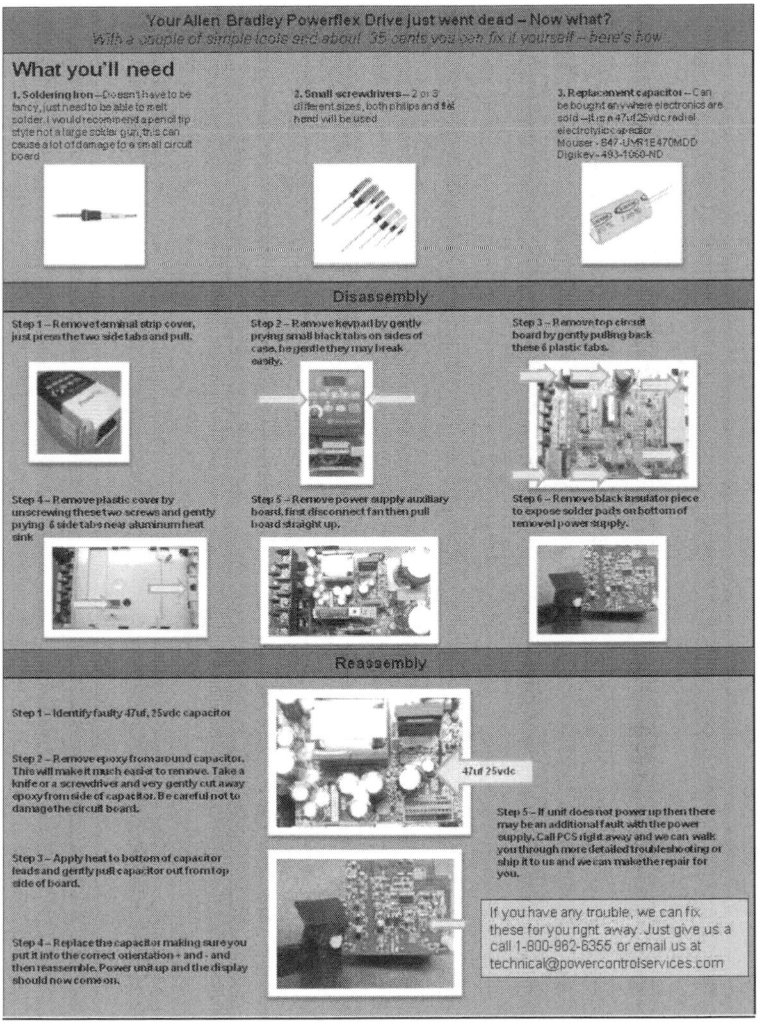

I have many more examples and details of this at:
www.walterbergeron.com

Thank you to our top 2011 Vendors

Mr. Bobby Musso
Community First Bank

Mr. Kevin Dubois
Technocopy

Mr. Jeff Ray
Abform

Congratulations to Mr. Bill Hebert - he won the free iPad 2

Mr. Bill Hebert of Control System Associates registered and attended our Open House that was held October 21st.

We want to personally thank Bill for his support over the years and hope he enjoys his new iPad2.

"You just made my wife very happy"

Well Bill, we hope you at least get to use it every once in a while at the very least. Enjoy.

Walter Bergeron – President of Power Control Services presents the iPad 2 to Mr. Bill Hebert of Control System Associates

Now this is a serious deal

Turkey Day Deal
$197.00 off
Safeline Lifetime Rebuild
-deadline 'Thanksgiving Day'

*CALL 1-800-962-6355 FOR AN RMA – TODAY

* Don't be the last person to get in on this deal

→ Priority Upgrade – done in 3 days
→ Free Shipping – UPS ground both ways
→ Lifetime Warranty – we back up our work forever!

Triple Guarantee

1. Guaranteed to work the first time, everytime
2. Guaranteed to never go obsolete
3. Guaranteed to never become Beyond Economical Repair

Just clowning around

USEFUL PHRASES AT WORK:

I like you. You remind me of when I was young and stupid.

I'm not being rude. You're just insignificant.

I'm already visualizing the duct tape over your mouth.

The fact that no one understands you doesn't mean you're an artist

Any connection between your reality and mine is purely coincidental

I have plenty of talent and vision. I just don't care.

I will always cherish the initial misconceptions I had about you.

No, my powers can only be used for good.

How about never? Is never good for you?

I'm really easy to get along with once you people learn to worship me

I'll try being nicer if you'll try being smarter.

Who me? I just wander from room to room.

You are validating my inherent mistrust of strangers.

I see you've set aside this special time to humiliate yourself in public.

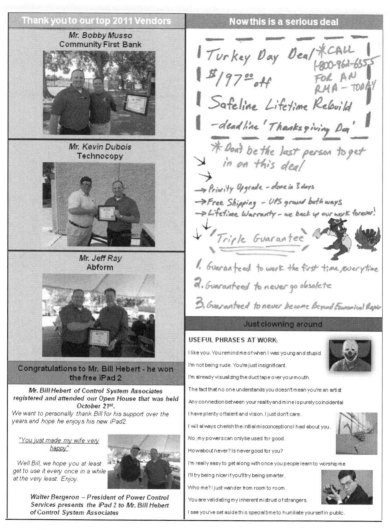

I have many more examples and details of this at:
www.walterbergeron.com

Fried Turkey!

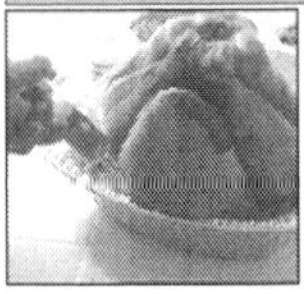

It ain't diet, it ain't low calorie, it ain't health food and it ain't paba free
But it sure tastes awesome!

Golden brown and delicious

Inject and marinate

Fry it up!

Here in Cajun Country, with all of the crawfish, crab and shrimp boils, a 30-quart pot, and 170,000 BTU cast iron burner are easy to get your hands on. We also needed 3-5 gallons of oil, a thermometer, and an injector to fry the turkey. Oh yeah – be sure careful, you don't want to start a fire in your yard.
If you are using frozen turkey, you will need a few days (following the package instructions) to thaw the turkey. Make sure it is completely thawed before frying. Remove the neck and giblets from the turkey. Cut away any excess skin at the neck opening and make sure there are no obstructions.
For our turkey marinade, I used one bottle of Zatarans Crab and Crawfish Boil, a very popular seafood boil. We injected the turkey getting plenty of the marinade into the meaty parts and let it marinate for 24 hours. Make sure you dry the turkey before immersion into the hot oil.

Remember that oil is flammable; you should never fry a turkey indoors. Make sure you are a safe distance from houses, overhangs, trees, leaves, or any other flammable objects. The cooking time is 3 to 3.5 minutes per pound. For a 10-pound turkey (3min/lb), that's about 30 minutes. For a 12-pound turkey (3.5min/lb) that's 42 minutes. The most accurate way to determine if your turkey is done is to use a meat thermometer. Stick it deep into the breast and thigh. An internal temperature of 180-190 degrees is recommended to be sure of eliminating bacteria. Using our hook on a pole, we removed the turkey after about 30 minutes of frying. It was an awesome golden brown turkey. It was delicious.
I think this is enough to get you started with your turkey. Overall, frying a turkey is fun and the turkey is awesome. Surprise your guests with a fried turkey. They are great any time of year.

Can I interest you in $100.00

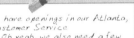

Do you know anyone that is looking for a great job? We have openings in our Atlanta, GA location as well as in Lafayette, LA location for Customer Service Representatives as well as Electronics Technicians. Oh yeah, we also need a few Outside Sales Representatives that operate nationwide. I am willing to pay you $100.00 for great candidates.

If we hire them and they last 90 days – I'm gonna send you 100 bucks for your troubles.

Outside Sales Representative

Outside Sales Representative needed in territories throughout the US. If you would like to be able to travel to client locations and determine their needs as well as assist them with selling Industrial Electronic Repair Services, we would really like to hear from you.

Customer Service Representative

Customer Service Representative to interface with clients via phone, email and in person. Be an expert in detailed computer database operation, must be able to learn extremely quickly and be an outstanding problem solver. Must be quick on your feet and have an outstanding attention to detail and willing to perform shipping and receiving duties as well as many clerical operations. This application process will test some of your problem solving skills so pay particular attention to the details of the process described on this page.

Electronic Technician

We are seeking highly skilled as well as entry level electronic technicians that have a strong desire to troubleshoot and repair industrial electronic equipment to the component level. An ideal candidate would have a strong foundation in electronics as well as get along with others in a close team atmosphere. They would have an exceptional level of attention to detail and a thirst for gaining new experiences and knowledge of a large range of electronic equipment operation.

For the full details - visit:
www.powercontrolservices.com/employment and just follow the instructions

I have many more examples and details of this at: www.walterbergeron.com

Day 35

11/3/11 – Thursday

- Sent out 4 more Platinum Level Rebuild packages – to date we have enrolled 16 of the 86 qualified service centers

- Sent out Lost Client Reactivation email #1 – got 3 responses right away from the email. It is so cool to get immediate response for my marketing efforts, email doesn't have a real high response rate but the immediate satisfaction is so very reassuring. This just feeds my energy for my marketing, days like this make it worth it.

- Organized marketing system manuals to help me not get so lost in all this paperwork and so I can see what in the world I am doing much more easily. I like things neat and clean and organized so I put everything into 1" 3 ring binders, looks so very impressive.

- Decided to repurpose lots of materials to other media – so everything I have done - newsletters, sales letters, etc….is going onto the website and emails and to give to walk in clients.

Day 36

11/4/11 – Friday

- I just received my Lost Client Reactivation campaign first response – an order for $1363.72 from a stupid boomerang letter. Can you believe that something as simple as a toy trinket from China and a slick little sales letter I didn't even write was going to get me over a thousand dollars! Unbelievable, truly crazy that this worked!

- New binders and organized the marketing system really well today with labels on the outside of them so now I can also physically see my efforts grow into a full fledged system and not just a bunch of disconnected marketing pieces.

- I started a customer service system so I know what to do on our business cards and scripts and have a convenient place to put the work we have done so far. I also let the customer service team know where this stuff is so they can access it and make revisions as they use it more and more.

- Redid marketing system calendar – to cover all of 2012

Day 37

11/7/11 – Monday

- I put the October and November newsletters online on the website and made them ready to email to all clients as well as put links on everyone's signatures in their emails. I want to think of more ways to re-purpose the content I created. I am also going to put up some brochure stands and put them at our customer service kiosk area so when our clients are waiting to pick up their equipment they can get to know a little more about us as well.

- Membership website for Infusionsoft products has been created through customer hub. I have no idea how to use this service, blind leap of faith – hope for the best.

- **ROADBLOCK – I had a great deal in the newsletter this month called the "Turkey Day Deal" man it is fantastic. I just didn't tell my customer service reps about it so when our clients called about it today I had to do some really fancy footwork and smooth talking to get our team up to speed. Lesson learned, give the team a copy of the newsletter BEFORE I send it out.**

Day 38

11/8/11 – Tuesday

- I created 2 information products so I can give them away for client contact information on the website. Research tells me that the two most popular topics are components and equipment by manufacture type. So the first e-book is called “Finding the Value of a Burned Resistor” and the second is “How to Repair the Most Common Failure of Allen Bradley Drives for 35 cents” We’ll give these a shot and see how they convert. We’ve got lots more topics and already mostly developed products from our normal operations so if these don’t work we’ll make more.

- I started a New Client Acquisition marketing system – I wrote the first sales letter and selected the first list for who I want to send it to.

- It seems every day I am getting more and more confident about the marketing and that I am doing the right thing. Really starting to feel so much better about this.

Day 39

11/9/11 – Wednesday

- Last coaching call with Jeff Wright. I really found his calls motivating to keep me moving forward. Every time I spoke with him I wanted to make sure I had a laundry list of implemented parts to our system so having someone hold me accountable, a coach, was truly invaluable to get me going and to keep me going.

- Completed web parts of new client campaign and I find I am picking up a lot of stuff really quickly with Joomla website.

- Bought mailing lists for new client campaign

- Ordered supplies form Office Depot for first letter of New Client Acquisition campaign

- Ordered some Russell Brunson products, the online marketing guru guy, products for online marketing. This is an area I am truly weak in and GKIC brags about this wonder kid. Let me make a little investment and see if there is anything I can use here.

Day 40

11/10/11 – Thursday

- Started new client letters, and this took most of the day as well as a lot of brain power. That was until I realized it was already done for me in the Magnetic Marketing binder. Why don't I just use the shortcuts GKIC gave me instead of trying to reinvent the wheel.

- So not only did I get the series of New Client letters mostly done but the campaign that these letters go into must have a grand finale' so I need to come up with what GKIC calls a "Shock and Awe" package. Right now that is a salesman making an appointment and taking the client to lunch, but that doesn't always work. Those appointments get cancelled at the last minute even after I pay for my salesman to travel across the country and conduct "lunch and learn" presentations, not to mention all the other costs. Need to find a more creative alternative that is going to knock these guys dead when they get it, whatever "IT" is.

Day 41

11/11/11 – Friday

- Stopped reinventing the wheel and completed New Client letters using the templates in Magnetic Marketing

- I wanted a new way to make our own language, new terminology like Starbucks did. I want to put ourselves into a category of one and change what we said as a company. So I changed the term – BER (Beyond Economical Repair) which is an industry term to Repair Exceptions (RE) and then we say before approval and after approval. See if this catches on with our clients.

- Then when we make a mistake, we also own it right away and give our clients a gift, even if they don't tell us we made a mistake. So if we found we made an error and whether our client knows we did or not, we send them an apology and a gift. Who else does that? NOBODY in our industry – That's a true category of 1 baby!

- **ROADBLOCK – The sign guys are at it again with a few more signs on the building and they need some hand holding time from me to tell them where to put them. I thought about telling them where to put something else, but decided against that comment in lieu of getting the job done quickly and pleasantly.**

Day 42

11/14/11 – Monday

- I spent the day doing lots of internet marketing training with Rusell Brunson websites and videos as well as Dustin Mathews and Dave VanHoose on stage presentations and video scripts and layout and offers.

- Sent out direct mail pieces Lost Client Reactivation #2. I am still folding the paper and stuffing the envelopes and putting on the stamps. This is really time consuming stuff. When I grow up and become a big boy I am going to hire this mundane stuff out.

- Sent out direct mail pieces New Client Acquisition #1

- My mind is mushy now so off to the gym I go

Day 43

11/15/11 – Tuesday

- Training, Training and more training. Good stuff and lots of notes. Next step is to take action on everything. Tomorrow is a new day!

- Module 12 – GKIC Max Mentoring Program online videos

- Modules 2- 6 Dot Com Secrets, many hours of video and introduced to so many different concepts and strategies. It's too much to absorb so I am going to take what I understand and implement what I can comprehend.

- **ROADBLOCK – We are having production time issues that we need to resolve. Another working lunch with the management team to get the evaluation time reduced to what we are promising. Not cool to break promises you put into your new marketing materials. We got it done but if they want to keep interrupting me then I am going to have to keep them working through their lunches. Although for some reason I keep paying them and on top of that I pay for the food. So who's getting the better end of this deal?**

Day 44

11/16/11 – Wednesday

- Russell Brunson training – all day long illuminati and Dot Com Secrets. So I am really about done with these multiple days of training. They are really great but I need to get some of this stuff done.

- The signs are up along the road and they are truly outrageous. Not a phone number or address on them, just instructions and answers to the most common client questions. The proof is going to be in the results. So we'll just count the number of clients that come to us because of these ridiculously over sized signs. This makes us unique and different than everyone else. This is the good is good enough philosophy at its' finest.

Day 45

11/17/11 – Thursday

- I completed the first Draft of December newsletter, this is much faster now that I have 2 of these already under my belt and a template to work from. Not starting from scratch is a great boost to the speed I can get this done in.

- I put together revision 1 of first information video products. Used camtasia and did the voice over. Went pretty smooth once I got the microphone to cooperate with me. Sometimes me and technology don't get along.

- Getting CBM, my website guys, to do website template for squeeze page. So today I became a big boy and I actually outsourced a task to someone that can do it better, faster and cheaper than I could if I did it myself. That allowed me to get much more done. I struggle with this daily to determine what is the best use of my time? It is always a balance between cash flow and highest productivity and best use of my time. There are so many gurus and books out there on time management that tell you to put a dollar value on your time, but I don't know how to guess what the hell that number is right now. So if I can do it super fast, like in a few hours, then I do it. If I need to learn how to do it first, then I outsource it for now.

Took a week off for Thanksgiving

and went to see in-laws in Idaho

More memories created to help motivate me

when the going gets tough.

Yeah!

Chapter Four

The Home Stretch

The year is almost over and I have tons more work to do. I have seen some results so far but I know I can achieve more. Maybe I am just too close to the action and what I see is just a small portion of the overall accomplishment. No time to ponder, just time to get more done. Month 3 is the home stretch to the end of the year. It is a time to wrap some things up and get them out the door and see if I can keep the results moving in the right direction.

2012 is almost here and I think this is the end of the world for some people, well if that happens then I am going out with one hell of a marketing system completed. I am going to face Armageddon with the best results I can possibly accomplish.

Day 46

11/28/11 – Monday

- Completed third draft of December newsletter, this means it's done. I won't spend another minute trying to make it any better. It's good, it's not perfect, but it's good and I even put a few new features into it that I swiped and deployed from GKIC. I hand wrote a monthly deal in crayon, actually paint pen, then scanned it and put it into the newsletter like a picture. It came out really neat, I might just use that more often if the clients like it. I also made that handwritten monthly deal the signature line of the emails for my customer service team, so now when they email clients I get to repurpose my content and my clients get a cool new deal in an unforgettable format.

- **ROADBLOCK – Thanksgiving break travel time was used as efficiently as possible. I made sure family time was family time, but there were a couple of days that I got up early and sat outside and listed to a CD or read a book. Sometimes you think more clearly when you haven't been at work for a few days.**

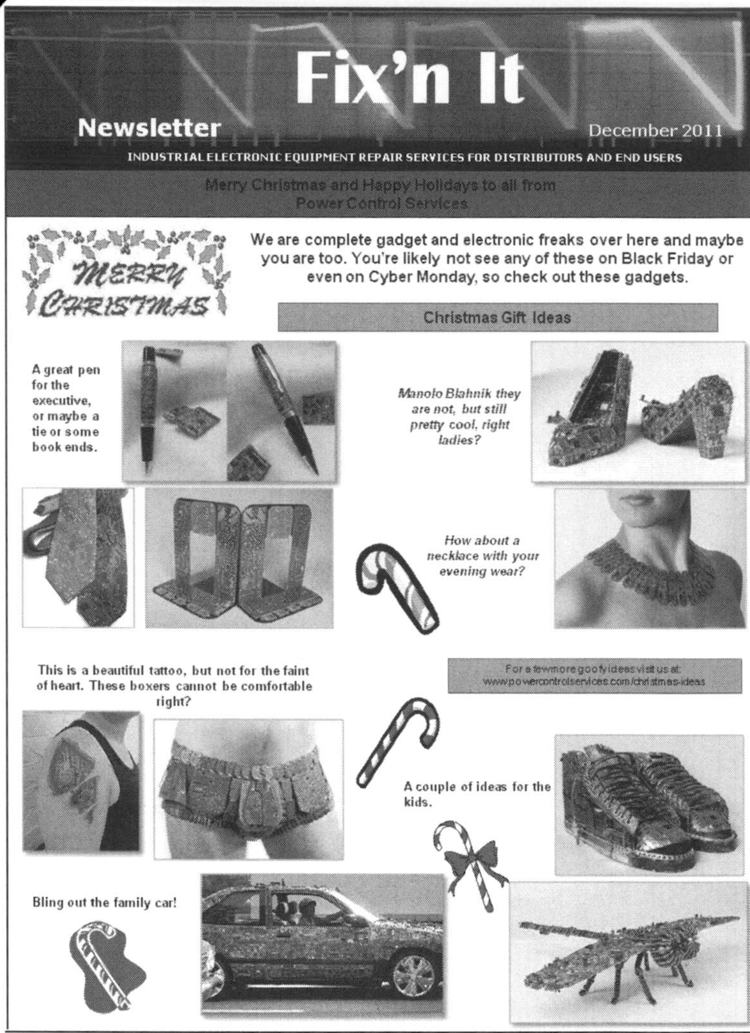
Fix'n It

Newsletter

December 2011

INDUSTRIAL ELECTRONIC EQUIPMENT REPAIR SERVICES FOR DISTRIBUTORS AND END USERS

Merry Christmas and Happy Holidays to all from
Power Control Services

MERRY CHRISTMAS

We are complete gadget and electronic freaks over here and maybe you are too. You're likely not see any of these on Black Friday or even on Cyber Monday, so check out these gadgets.

Christmas Gift Ideas

A great pen for the executive, or maybe a tie or some book ends.

Manolo Blahnik they are not, but still pretty cool, right ladies?

How about a necklace with your evening wear?

This is a beautiful tattoo, but not for the faint of heart. These boxers cannot be comfortable right?

For a fewmore goofyideas visit us at:
www.powercontrolservices.com/christmas-ideas

A couple of ideas for the kids.

Bling out the family car!

I have many more examples and details of this at:
www.walterbergeron.com

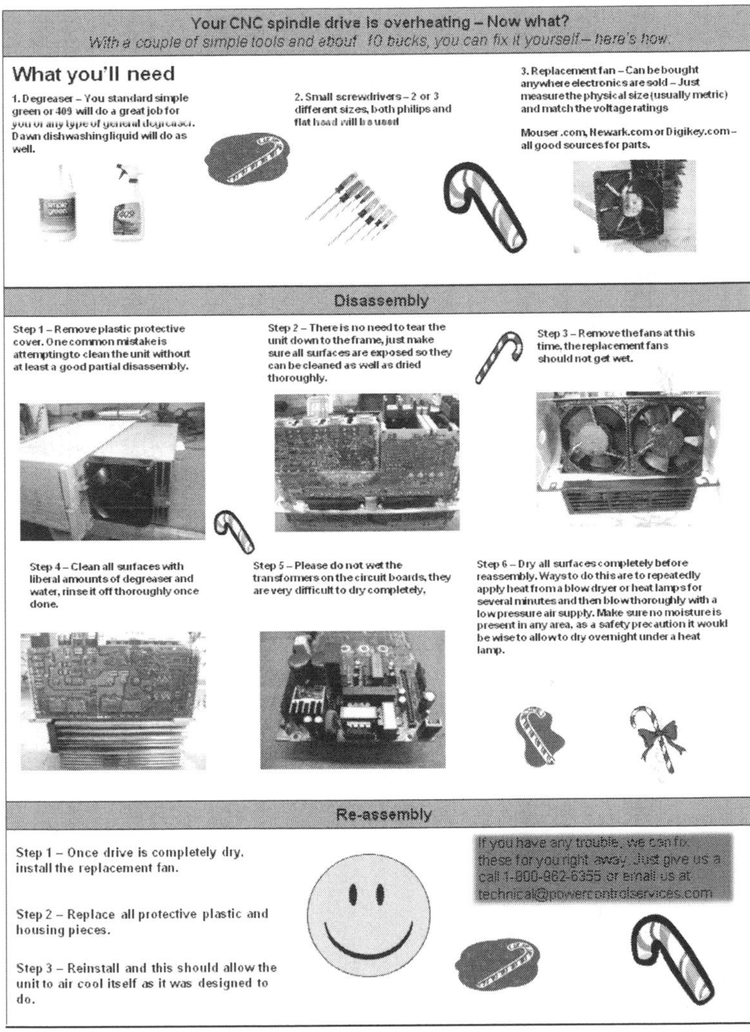

Your CNC spindle drive is overheating – Now what?

With a couple of simple tools and about 10 bucks, you can fix it yourself – here's how.

What you'll need

1. Degreaser – You standard simple green or 409 will do a great job for you or any type of general degreaser. Dawn dishwashing liquid will do as well.

2. Small screwdrivers – 2 or 3 different sizes, both philips and flat head will be used

3. Replacement fan – Can be bought anywhere electronics are sold – Just measure the physical size (usually metric) and match the voltage ratings

Mouser.com, Newark.com or Digikey.com – all good sources for parts.

Disassembly

Step 1 – Remove plastic protective cover. One common mistake is attempting to clean the unit without at least a good partial disassembly.

Step 2 – There is no need to tear the unit down to the frame, just make sure all surfaces are exposed so they can be cleaned as well as dried thoroughly.

Step 3 – Remove the fans at this time, the replacement fans should not get wet.

Step 4 – Clean all surfaces with liberal amounts of degreaser and water, rinse it off thoroughly once done.

Step 5 – Please do not wet the transformers on the circuit boards, they are very difficult to dry completely.

Step 6 – Dry all surfaces completely before reassembly. Ways to do this are to repeatedly apply heat from a blow dryer or heat lamps for several minutes and then blow thoroughly with a low pressure air supply. Make sure no moisture is present in any area, as a safety precaution it would be wise to allow to dry overnight under a heat lamp.

Re-assembly

Step 1 – Once drive is completely dry, install the replacement fan.

Step 2 – Replace all protective plastic and housing pieces.

Step 3 – Reinstall and this should allow the unit to air cool itself as it was designed to do.

If you have any trouble, we can fix these for you right away. Just give us a call 1-800-982-6355 or email us at technical@powercontrolservices.com

I have many more examples and details of this at:
www.walterbergeron.com

I have many more examples and details of this at:
www.walterbergeron.com

Going Above and Beyond our Competitors
E-Book Library – Free Downloads!

Repair Catalog – almost 1000 pages of equipment part numbers. We can repair equipment from over 15,000 different manufacturers and over 300,000 different part numbers. We are now the largest 100 dedicated repair facility in the United States!

Independent Representative Selling System – Training you to become a top performing salesman in the Industrial Electronic Repair business. Focus our services on your clients to achieve the best sales levels you've ever had with a proven marketing system.

Distributor Selling System – Training you to become a top performing distributor in the Industrial Electronic Repair business. Focus our services on your clients to achieve the best sales levels you've ever had with a proven marketing system.

Burnt Resistor Value Determination – For the serious electronic technician that has run into the resistor that is not easy to identify due to significant overheating. We show you the detailed ways to find the value every time.

6 Secrets to getting expert industrial electronic repair for less– The top 6 ways to make sure you pay the very least for your industrial electronic repairs, no matter who you use for your repairs.

Allen Bradley PowerFlex 4/40 Repair – For the maintenance personnel that has a drive that won't power up. This is a .35 cent fix for that most common problem.

For the full details on all of our ebooks visit: www.powercontrolservices.com/ebooks and just fill out your first name and email and we'll get it emailed to you right away.

What our clients are saying about us

Have had many circuit board repairs done with PCS. Overall, I would say their repair correspondence and quoting are great, customer service is good and turn around time is fairly consistent. I have had success using PCS.

Scott Asmann
N. Sioux City, SD

You guys and gals are the best. And that's why we send all of our repairs to Power Control Services. I am faxing over the signed quote right now.

Best Regards,
James Hanson
Eagle River, AK

You guys did a great job, we really appreciated the speed you did it for us. I am telling our locations in Florida and Houston about your terrific services.

Thanks,
Steve McCauley
Kansas City, MO

I have many more examples and details of this at:
www.walterbergeron.com

Day 47

11/29/11 – Tuesday

- Worked on new client direct mail letter #2, again I went back to Magnetic Marketing industrial sales letters for examples and I think I have a way to put the video into a format my clients can see without them having to use their own computer as my secret weapon for this campaign.

- Printed 300 envelopes for December newsletter and 500 newsletters. I am still folding these things by hand, but this is the last time. I found a folding machine on ebay and it is on its' way today. I need to get these out soon so it won't do me any good today, but just knowing it's on its way gives me a little satisfaction that my hands won't need to endure this torture again. Hands don't fail me now! Massive action.

Day 48

11/30/11 – Wednesday

- Completed new client direct mail letter #2

- Completed local repairs web page, Things are still easy to do with Joomla and I am glad I have an easy to go to resource in case I have anything complex I want done with the website.

- Printed new client letters – 175 of them 3 pages each. I used my own yellow toner but a more cost effective way to do this will be to find a good yellow paper to print this on. Yellow tone $150.00, yellow paper $20.00 – Doesn't take a rocket science to figure this one out.

- Completed Tyson web portal video and sent schedule monthly email campaign

- Updated Tyson webpage with video and pdf of web portal instructions

- Scheduled eNewsletter for email on Friday 10:00 am. Infusionsoft sure makes this easy to do. Point and click.

Day 49

12/1/11 – Thursday

- Folded and stuffed envelopes for 476 newsletters – took over 4 hours – CANT WAIT TO GET THAT FOLDING MACHINE – my hands are killing me!

- Worked on ebooks webpage. I place all of our current ebooks in one location so I can refer to that page in the newsletter.

- Also made multiple squeeze pages to send client to the ebook page as a way to capture their contact information. After the ebook I will follow up with a diagnostic questionnaire so we can see what their needs are and then send them to the automated webinar.

- **ROADBLOCK – I just looked at the KPI's for the upcoming month and it is starting off as our best month of the entire year. This is supposed to be a slow time of the year for manufacturing plants with holiday shutdown last week and vacations. My VP of Operations had been out on vacation all week and I think I need to go a rally the troops for a few minutes after seeing what they are in for this month.**

Day 50

12/2/11 – Friday

- Started 2 new newsletters Platinum and Tyson. We have different clients that I need to speak to in a different way. After a couple of newsletters already started I think I can do these pretty quickly once I get the initial format completed.

- Folded and stuffed 2nd direct mail piece for new client machine shops. Used the new folding machine, this is a life saver and my fingers appreciated every minute of not having to fold those letters.

- More and more people are stopping by because of the signs. We are going to need someone in the office full time so I don't have to stop what I am doing every 20 minutes to answer questions and count the people coming in off the street. These things are really working.

Day 51

12/5/11 – Monday

- Mailed December newsletters, I had the mailman actually come in and pick them up this time instead of making a trip to the post office. He was happy to do it and I was happy for him to do it too.

- Mailed direct mail piece #2 – machine shops (337) area code

- I used some information we used to train our own technicians and completed 2 new info products – Capacitor discharge and Fuse replacement. The other ebooks have had some conversions so I made two new ones to help build up our library of information products for our clients.

- Completed final draft of Tyson and Platinum newsletters. I am getting so much faster at these newsletters, pick a theme, download a few pictures, write some content, throw it into power point and presto – you've got a newsletter.

Day 52

12/6/11 – Tuesday

- I touched up Tyson and Platinum newsletters – I just realized after looking at the list of recipients of these newsletters that there is some overlap in clients so I may need to make them very different to avoid any confusion.

- Worked on audio interview questions and answers – National account manager has first person lined up for me and I'll get it done later on today

- Got Fiverr guy to write a Safeline article – will see how this goes to see if I continue to use this service

- Did first client interview, went great and he was totally flattered to do it. I sent him a copy of the CD, a framed thank you letter and a CD Case with this picture on it as well as his company name.

Day 53

12/7/11 – Wednesday

- Cleaned up Platinum and Tyson lists in Infusionsoft 225 and 74 respectively. These lists are going to get the best of me, I think I have gone through most of my clients so far thank goodness.

- Printed up Tyson and Platinum envelopes. I think I might want to invest in a better printer that can handle more than 10 envelopes at a time, this is surely one slow process to feed these things in one small handful at a time.

- Worked on 2012 marketing calendar. It's coming along well, I am taking what I have done over the last couple of months and using that as what I am going to do next year. A good guideline and of course it will need to be revised.

- I feel like the energizer bunny, I keep going and going. Massive action helps to build momentum.

Day 54

12/8/11 – Thursday

- I completed Tyson newsletters for December, I am going to put this same information onto the Tyson webpage as well as into an email to all Tyson account managers. This is a great way to communicate with them in multiple ways and give them the details of how to access their accounts on the website new web portal we developed for them

- Worked on participation reports to plan next year marketing calendar. Now I have an entire book giving detailed numbers on how effective the marketing has been. I need to go look at the Dan Kennedy book for ruthless management, it has a few numbers I think might be useful to calculate or even to start to accumulate so we can more accurately judge what we are doing.

- **ROADBLOCK – I haven't had any time for Christmas shopping so I took a long lunch today and got some of it done. The rest will have to be done online and I'll talk to my shipping and receiving people to make sure that anything that is marked for me personally is left unopened and they come get me immediately OR ELSE! Since Jana and I work together I need to get to the boxes before she can see what they are. Santa Clause needs to have some surprises.**

Day 55

12/9/11 – Friday

- Mailed 74 Tyson newsletters, this is so much easier with that folding machine. There are some other areas I need to cover in this newsletter and include in the future. I really don't have any call to action or offer in this version of it. There needs to be a way to make this more interactive to the Tyson sales people so we can engage them and make them more active with us. Word find maybe, giveaways possibly though I have to be really careful not to violate their gift policy and get their employees into trouble. Need to give this more thought.

- Worked on client participation for 2011 so I can see the returns on what time and money I have invested into all this marketing stuff

Day 56

12/12/11 – Monday

- Mailed all of Platinum newsletters. The same thoughts I had about the Tyson newsletter apply to Platinum clients. They need more interactivity and not just a monthly report of their activity. There is a little more room with these clients for gift giving but we could also add some incentives and monthly contests with them to increase response and this will also be a great place to showcase successes and maybe even infuse some competition in the levels of participation they have with us.

- Completed third direct mail piece for machine shops (337) area code (173 of them). Recorded the responses we have so far in the "Results Notebook" as I have affectionately named it. Will study this in more detail with the numbers from Dan's ruthless management book.

Day 57

12/13/11 – Tuesday

- Printed envelopes for 337 area code machine shops third direct mail piece as well as folded all the letters and stuffed the envelopes and mailed all pieces to them.

- I think I just found the way to shock and awe our clients at the end of the new client campaign. Since we already have the video developed and it is converting well on the website, let's use it on a digital picture frame we send to our clients. We can send instructions and have them plug it in and it will play the video for them. We can send the contract with the video picture frame and ship it in one of our standard boxes and this will be completely different from what anyone else is doing. This would be completely outrageous if we can find an economical way to get a frame that will play video and then have them ship it back to us when they are done.

Day 58

12/14/11 Wednesday

- Russell Brunson and Dustin and Dave Training all day long

- Did more research on the shock and awe video player and found one of them on Amazon for $60 so I ordered it, should be here tomorrow so I can experiment with it and see how the video quality is. The more I think about it the more I want to make it like a mission impossible video, it will self-destruct at the end of this message if they don't act on the instructions. If there is a way to battery power it and make it last for at least a couple of hours and not need a case of batteries to use it, that might just work.

Day 59

12/15/11 – Thursday

- Began continuity program planning for our end user clients. The Platinum program will need to evolve into the continuity program for our sales clients, we'll add a $997 charge to them, but for now as long as they are producing we'll let them have "access" to the program for free. In the future once we fill up the 50 slots we said we would do we can charge new clients the fee to enroll. This will give us guaranteed income from new clients and the program will have a track record of success already so we can more easily sell it to our new clients. Brilliant Walter – way to swipe and deploy a great idea from GKIC and make it your own!
- For our end users we'll call the program our Gold Level Repair Program and give them better service than our drop by one time only type of clients. This will make them feel more exclusive with us and give us a $497 per month continuity fee. Once again, you are a genius – or just a thief for swiping and deploying these ideas from GKIC . Massive action today.

Day 60

12/16/11 – Friday

- Working on membership continuity program for end users. It is called the Gold Level Repair program and gives them tremendously more value and service than if they are not a member at all. They'll have 24/7 access to our technical service department, their own exclusive access number to call in for support. Faster turnaround time for repairs and head of the line privileges. Their own parking spots right out front and we'll give them top notch service because they are enrolled into such a special program with us.

- My video player is here and I fitted it with D cell batteries and it plays for about 3 hours which will be plenty of time to view the video. I also cut the power cord and will permanently mount it inside a box. This will make it useless to the end user after they have watched our video so we'll include a prepaid shipping label inside it and they'll send it back to us with a signed contract. I should look into a reusable case now that they will be shipping it back to us as well as change the video to give them the final instructions.

Day 61

12/19/11 – Monday

- Began putting together the automated webinar presentation for Platinum program

- Last night I did a mock up of the video box and Jana vetoed the cardboard box idea and found me a box on Amazon that I can use that looks industrial and can fit the video player inside, should get is after I get back from vacation to play with it.

- We also listened to the video and the sound is great as well as the video plays great, we had to format the video a little differently to make it play smoother but we got the kinks worked out of it I think. I can't wait to see how it looks inside the industrial case Jana picked out. Jana also decided that since we are coming up on Mardi Gras season, yes it is an entire season here in Louisiana, that we should include something that shows a bit of our culture and so we found out that the box will be able to hold a King Cake inside it that we would include one with our shock and awe box. This will truly be something they have never seen before Nowhere in the country is anyone doing anything like this as a shock and awe marketing package.

Took time off for Holidays

Created more memories

to give me the proof this effort is paying off.

Day 62

12/27/11 – Tuesday

- Completed automated webinar and placed on website. Now getting feedback from webinar participants

- Put the video player into the box and permanently mounted it inside, this thing is absolutely amazing looking. It is the shock and awe we were looking for and I can't wait to see how it performs as the secret weapon in our outrageous new client campaigns we are doing.

- I think it is going to overcome some of the roadblocks we are hitting with outside sales staff getting cancelled appointments to sell our Platinum Level Rebuild Program. This will quickly get past the gatekeepers because these clients get packages all day long so this won't surprise them when they get something from UPS or FedEx. Then when they see that the outside of the box says "Perishable goods open immediately" they are going to open it right away. Then the video will start to play automatically because we put a hinge activated micro switch. The video instructs them to eat the king cake, watch the video, sign the contract and send it back to us. This is truly an industry changing moment for us and our soon to be clients. Holy Cow thank you GKIC for this kind of an impact.

- **MASSIVE ACTION, GOOD IS GOOD ENOUGH AND SIMULTANEOUS IMPLEMENTATION PAID OFF IN A MAJOR WAY!**

Day 63

12/28/11 – Wednesday

- Completed first draft of January newsletter and making newsletters quickly is becoming a skill of mine. We now produce 4 different newsletters and we print them, email them, publish them on the website, hand them to our walk-in clients and ship them in the boxes of repaired equipment back to our clients. We are experts at making this work for us in as many ways as we can.

- Getting front lobby video set up and running now that our signs are up and producing 5.6 new clients per week. These signs are tremendously advantageous to us. I don't know why we didn't do them months ago – oh yeah, we didn't know how to do them months ago that's why.

- We also have the walk in client script and information capture forms in the front lobby. As well as we put them in the receiving area for our customer service team to use when new clients show up back there with equipment to drop off.

2012 Fix'n It Newsletter

HAPPY NEW YEAR

January 2012

INDUSTRIAL ELECTRONIC EQUIPMENT REPAIR SERVICES FOR DISTRIBUTORS AND END USERS

Whatever phrase you prefer or language you speak, Happy New Year!

Like it or not 2012 has begun and this is usually the time you are starting to waiver on those many resolutions you made and hopefully you started them on January 1st. I'm sure you are still going strong and there's no way you are going to fall off the wagon. I'll bet everyone around you is trying to help you out and make sure you keep your resolutions.

Sorry, but I am not one of those guys since I have already dropped out of a couple of my resolutions. I came up with some great excuses why I stopped (or started again, depending on what my resolution was). So if you are looking for some great reasons to quit then let me help you out and give you 20 fantastic reasons that you can't keep your resolutions.

Top 20 Best Excuses To Quit Your New Years Resolution

1. If only I had more time
2. If only I could afford it
3. If only I could eat healthier
4. If only I could stick with it
5. If only I wasn't hungry all the time
6. If only I didn't have kids
7. If only I knew how to do it
8. If only I were younger
9. If only I had somebody to help me
10. If only the economy was better
11. If only I had been given a shot
12. If only I had better genetics
13. If only I didn't have so much weight to lose
14. If only I didn't have to try so hard
15. If only I hadn't failed in the past
16. If only I could just catch a break
17. If only I had more confidence
18. If only I were luckier
19. If only I had a workout partner
20. If only I could just get started

Top 10 ways to weasel out of resolutions by saying what you really meant

I will lose weight *(by buying an Xbox 360 Kinect and playing more video games)*
I will stop eating chocolate *(while watching biggest loser)*
I will save more money *(by not giving to charity)*
I will get more education *(in the subject of football)*
I will find a better job *(by updating my resume at work and then forging my bosses signature for a reference)*
I will earn a better wage *(by working fewer hours but still getting paid for them, like using facebook at work)*
I will drink less beer *(while driving to work)*
I will stop smoking *(in front of people that I told I would quit smoking)*
I will exercise more *(by considering everything an exercise like every bite of a donut is considered 1 rep)*
I will be more charitable *(by giving myself things that I think others should give me)*

IN THIS ISSUE

Get it all online at:
www.powercontrolservices.com/Newsletter-January2012

Platinum Level Rebuild Program

All kidding aside, 2012 has got to be the year you RESOLVE to get involved in a unique program that is not offered anywhere else and make this year **the most successful year** you have ever had selling a service to your clients that they will beg you to offer to them. Go immediately to www.powercontrolservices.com/platinum and watch an extraordinary video about something that will make your 2012 unbelievable!

I have many more examples and details of this at:
www.walterbergeron.com

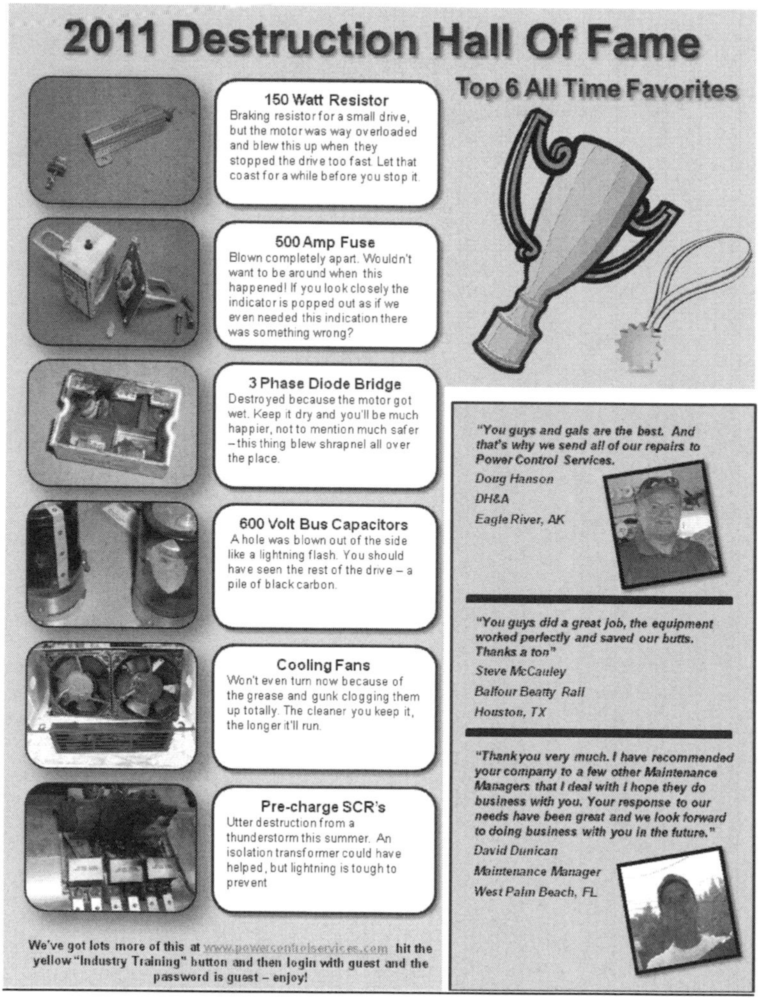

2011 Destruction Hall Of Fame
Top 6 All Time Favorites
150 Watt Resistor
Braking resistor for a small drive, but the motor was way overloaded and blew this up when they stopped the drive too fast. Let that coast for a while before you stop it.
500 Amp Fuse
Blown completely apart. Wouldn't want to be around when this happened! If you look closely the indicator is popped out as if we even needed this indication there was something wrong?
3 Phase Diode Bridge
Destroyed because the motor got wet. Keep it dry and you'll be much happier, not to mention much safer – this thing blew shrapnel all over the place.
600 Volt Bus Capacitors
A hole was blown out of the side like a lightning flash. You should have seen the rest of the drive – a pile of black carbon.
Cooling Fans
Won't even turn now because of the grease and gunk clogging them up totally. The cleaner you keep it, the longer it'll run.
Pre-charge SCR's
Utter destruction from a thunderstorm this summer. An isolation transformer could have helped, but lightning is tough to prevent
"You guys and gals are the best. And that's why we send all of our repairs to Power Control Services.
Doug Hanson
DH&A
Eagle River, AK
"You guys did a great job, the equipment worked perfectly and saved our butts. Thanks a ton"
Steve McCauley
Balfour Beatty Rail
Houston, TX
"Thankyou very much. I have recommended your company to a few other Maintenance Managers that I deal with I hope they do business with you. Your response to our needs have been great and we look forward to doing business with you in the future."
David Dunican
Maintenance Manager
West Palm Beach, FL
We've got lots more of this at www.powercontrolservices.com hit the yellow "Industry Training" button and then login with guest and the password is guest – enjoy!

I have many more examples and details of this at:
www.walterbergeron.com

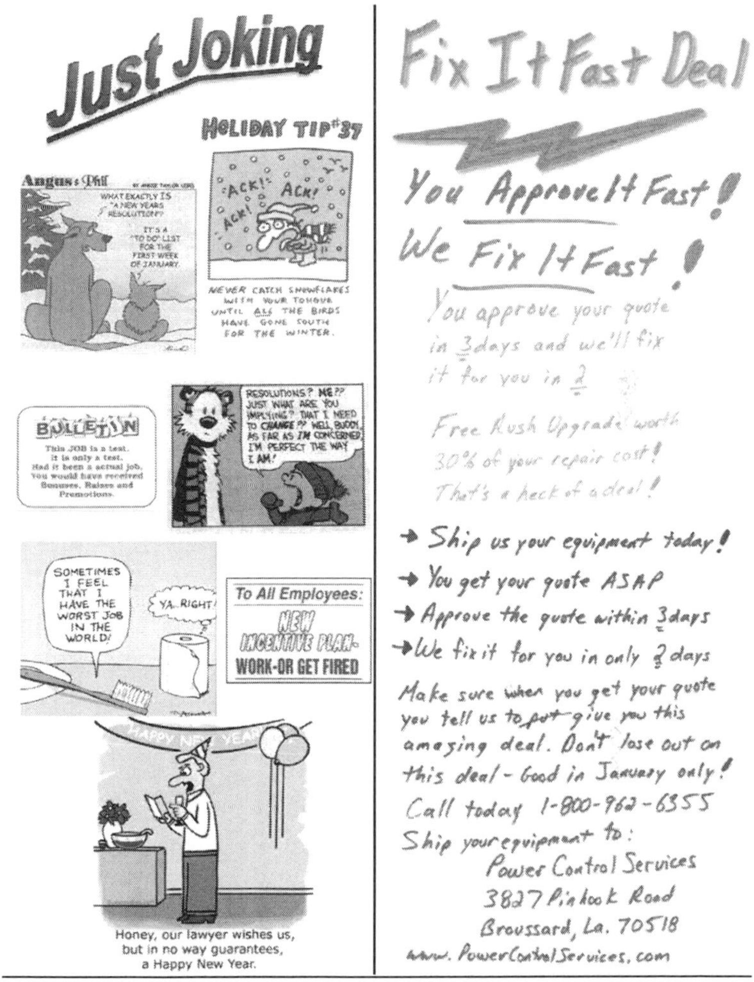

I have many more examples and details of this at:
www.walterbergeron.com

2012 $10.00 for your opinion

gift CARD

$10.00 for your opinion

Happy New Year!

Can I pay you for your opinion?
Can I send you a $10.00 gift card to Best Buy for speaking your mind?

You get to speak your mind and we make it super duper easy. The good, the bad and the ugly are all welcome. My name is Walter Bergeron and I am the President of Power Control Services and I want to know how we are doing and I want to pay you for telling me.

Here's how it works:

1. Speak your mind by checking off the boxes. Fax it to me or go to www.powercontrolservices.com/speak-your-mind to fill it out online. I will use the best ones for our marketing materials and the bad ones I'll use to make us better. If I can find you on the social websites I'll grab your photo as well.
2. I will send you a $10.00 gift card for your troubles. No drawing, no limited supplies, no catch – you send me a comment, I send you a gift card – simple and easy and no catch!

Who should I make out the gift card to:

Name:________________________

Company:______________________

Where should I send it to:

Address:_______________________

City:__________________________

State:_______________Zip:_______

What kind of equipment did you send us?

- ☐ Drive
- ☐ Display
- ☐ PLC
- ☐ Other

Did you take advantage of our Free shipping?

- ☐ Yes, you provided me with a UPS Ground account number
- ☐ No, Could you get me more information about it immediately and Email it to me at:

____

Did you get your quote fast enough?

- ☐ Yes, faster than expected
- ☐ Just in time
- ☐ Would have preferred it to be faster
- ☐ Way too slow

Was the price we quoted you a fair price?

- ☐ Yes, less than expected
- ☐ Just right
- ☐ Would have preferred it to be cheaper
- ☐ Way too expensive

Was your repair completed fast enough?

- ☐ Yes, faster than expected
- ☐ Just in time
- ☐ Would have preferred it to be faster
- ☐ Way too slow

Did the equipment work like expected?

- ☐ Yes, it's still running now
- ☐ Haven't put it in service yet
- ☐ Not sure, will let you know
- ☐ No, can you get me some help

Would you use us again for future equipment breakdowns?

- ☐ Yes, of course
- ☐ If the price is right, you'll get my work
- ☐ Might look at other options
- ☐ No, I have started using someone else

Did you know you could get involved in a program where you'll never have to pay for another repair again – ever!?

- ☐ Yes, I am already a member of the Platinum Level Rebuild Program
- ☐ I am aware of this amazing program but not yet a member
- ☐ No, Could you get me more information about it immediately and Email it to me at ______________________________

Now fax this over to 1-877-856-8488 or go to www.powercontrolservices.com/speak-your-mind to complete this online and then I'll immediately get your gift card on its way.

I have many more examples and details of this at: www.walterbergeron.com

Day 64

12/29/11 – Thursday

- Completed second draft of January newsletter and it went very fast and very smooth. It is sure great to have these templates and months of experience now. This will be our first month with a CD insert into the newsletter like GKIC monthly gold CD with a client testimonial as well as technical interview with an expert in the field, my own technicians.
- New information request form for newsletter to get updated client contact information as well as testimonials and referrals. We are really putting these newsletters to work and last month we got our first viral response, a client reusing the newsletter for other co-workers to respond, that is amazing to get something as simple as a newsletter to help us build our list as well as testimonials and referrals.

Chapter Five

The Ride to Marketer of the Year

Now after that initial 90 days I certainly didn't stop what I was doing but I did take a breath and begin to look at the numbers of what I accomplished in extreme detail so that I could determine what was effective and what was not

<u>Website – With Information capture free report</u>

Content :
Front page with "Learn these 6 crucial secrets you need to know before you send your repairs to anyone!" and Infusionsoft follow up campaign
Results:
43 New end user clients resulting in $38,234.29 in sales to date with a Lifetime Client Value of $166,946.21
4 New distributor clients resulting in $3,560.95 in sales to date with a Lifetime Client Value of $138,303.80
Cost Per Lead –$75.32 per lead
Cost Per Sale – $43.60 per sale currently and will go to $5.17 over client lifetime

About Us | Our Process | Technical Support | Downloads | Contact Us
Electronic Repairs
Part Number Search
Industry Training
Technical Library
Client Log-In
Get Your Repair Status
Reseller Opportunities
Get Paid For Your Repairs
Power Control Services: PowerControlServices.com - Industrial Electronic Repair
AC Drive Repairs - DC Drive Repairs - Servo Drive Repairs - Circuit Board Repairs - Power Supply Repairs
You won't pay for shipping - just send us a purchase order pre-approving the repair price
You won't pay for evaluation - we'll let you know exactly what we find wrong with your equipment before you pay a dime
Repairs are guaranteed to work - we don't just repair your equipment, we do a complete teardown and rebuild to a like new condition. Your equipment will be serviced by factory trained technicians and we'll back it up with a lifetime warranty.
You get 6 choices for service - the factory and everyone else will give you 2 ways to repair your equipment, we give you 6 ways to meet your needs. Stop being restricted by their limited capabilities and get repairs done the way you want them done.
You'll pay so much less for so much more - if you buy new equipment when your equipment fails then you are paying way too much and getting way too little. We'll repair it for 50% less than new and you get a complete rebuild, a lifetime warranty and a better price - this is unbeatable!
PICK IT You choose how fast you want us to get your equipment back to you and what you want done to it. Now you have many more choices than you have ever had before.
PRICE IT Call us and we'll do an RMA for you - OR - Click on the orange "Electronic Repairs" button above and do everything online
SHIP IT
SEE WHAT OUR CLIENTS ARE SAYING ABOUT US
Learn these 6 crucial secrets you need to know before you send your repairs to anyone!
We'll send the 6 secrets to you right away!
First Name
Email
Submit

4 Critical Reasons
DISTRIBUTOR
BURNT
RESISTOR
VALUE
DETERMINATION
Allen Bradley
6 Secrets

Exterior Signs – 21 signs over 1500 sf

Content:

Most commonly asked clients questions with call to action and deadline

Results:

We considered this outrageous because of the sheer size and number and we used the idea that the casinos use along the freeway - multiple signs with successive messages.

29 New clients resulting in $44,464.82 in sales to date with a Lifetime Client Value of $260,901.98

Cost Per Lead –$551.72 per lead

Cost Per Sale - $84.90 per sale currently and will go to $24.85 if we replace with new signs every year PLUS clients have increased frequency by 275%

I have many more examples and details of this at: www.walterbergeron.com

Open House – Niche of 551 local end user clients invited and 18 vendors

Results:

We considered this outrageous because we had local bank VP's attend and put on a fish fry with music and lots of vendor giveaways.

Immediate daily sales increase of $4,700.00

Cost Per Lead –$.48 per lead

Cost Per Sale – $104.28 per sale currently and will go to $2.78 over lifetime of client

Distributor Newsletter – Niche of 661 distributor clients

Content:

40% Deals and business related news, 60% humor and fun stuff

Results:

We considered this outrageous because of the colors and humor we put into every issue.

Reactivated 1 client resulting in $30,000 job

Monthly deals taken advantage of $47,000 in sales

Cost Per Lead –$48.48 per lead

Cost Per Sale – $14.28 per sale currently and will go to $.28 over lifetime of client

End User Newsletter – Niche of 163 end user clients

Content:

40% Deals and business related news, 60% humor and fun stuff tailored to maintenance personnel

Results:

No new clients or sales can be directly attributed to this newsletter

Cost Per Lead –$infinite per lead

Cost Per Sale – $infinite per sale currently

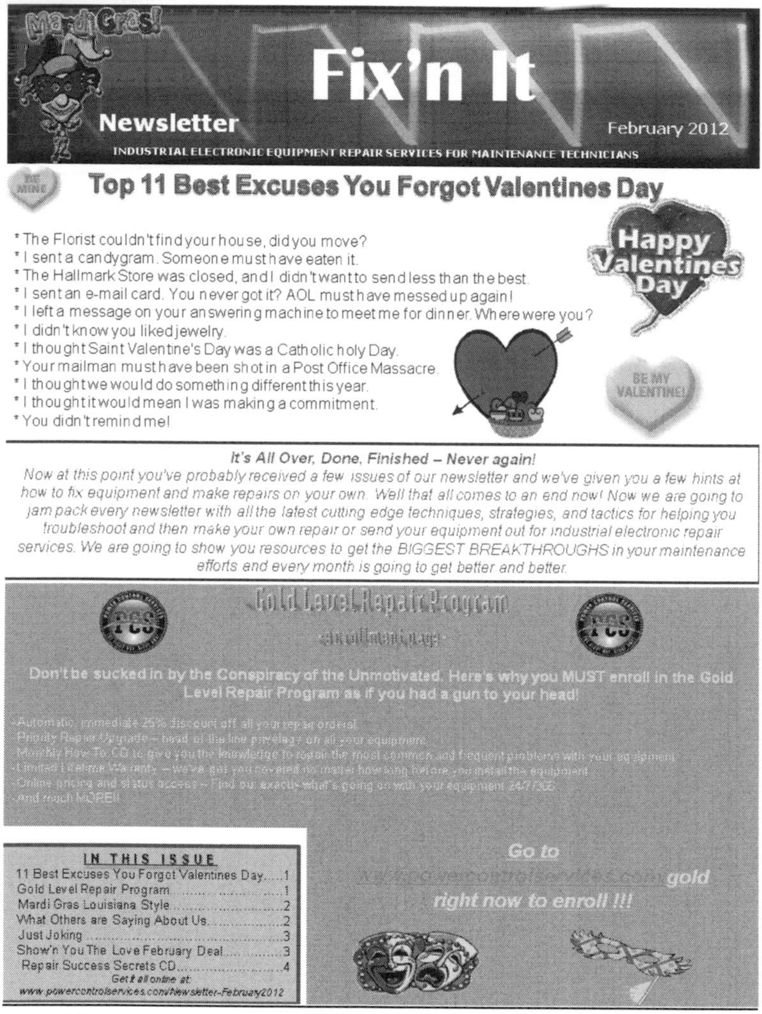

Mardi Gras!

Fix'n It

Newsletter

February 2012

INDUSTRIAL ELECTRONIC EQUIPMENT REPAIR SERVICES FOR MAINTENANCE TECHNICIANS

Top 11 Best Excuses You Forgot Valentines Day

* The Florist couldn't find your house, did you move?
* I sent a candygram. Someone must have eaten it.
* The Hallmark Store was closed, and I didn't want to send less than the best.
* I sent an e-mail card. You never got it? AOL must have messed up again!
* I left a message on your answering machine to meet me for dinner. Where were you?
* I didn't know you liked jewelry.
* I thought Saint Valentine's Day was a Catholic holy Day.
* Your mailman must have been shot in a Post Office Massacre.
* I thought we would do something different this year.
* I thought it would mean I was making a commitment.
* You didn't remind me!

It's All Over, Done, Finished – Never again!

Now at this point you've probably received a few issues of our newsletter and we've given you a few hints at how to fix equipment and make repairs on your own. Well that all comes to an end now! Now we are going to jam pack every newsletter with all the latest cutting edge techniques, strategies, and tactics for helping you troubleshoot and then make your own repair or send your equipment out for industrial electronic repair services. We are going to show you resources to get the BIGGEST BREAKTHROUGHS in your maintenance efforts and every month is going to get better and better.

Gold Level Repair Program

Don't be sucked in by the Conspiracy of the Unmotivated. Here's why you MUST enroll in the Gold Level Repair Program as if you had a gun to your head!

-Automatic, immediate 25% discount off all your repair orders!
-Priority Repair Upgrade – head of the line privelage on all your equipment
-Monthly How-To CD to give you the knowledge to repair the most common and frequent problems with your equipment
-Limited Lifetime Warranty – we've got you covered no matter how long before you install the equipment
-Online pricing and status access – Find out exactly what's going on with your equipment 24/7/365
-And much MORE!!

IN THIS ISSUE

Get it all online at:
www.powercontrolservices.com/Newsletter-February2012

Go to
gold right now to enroll !!!

I have many more examples and details of this at:
www.walterbergeron.com

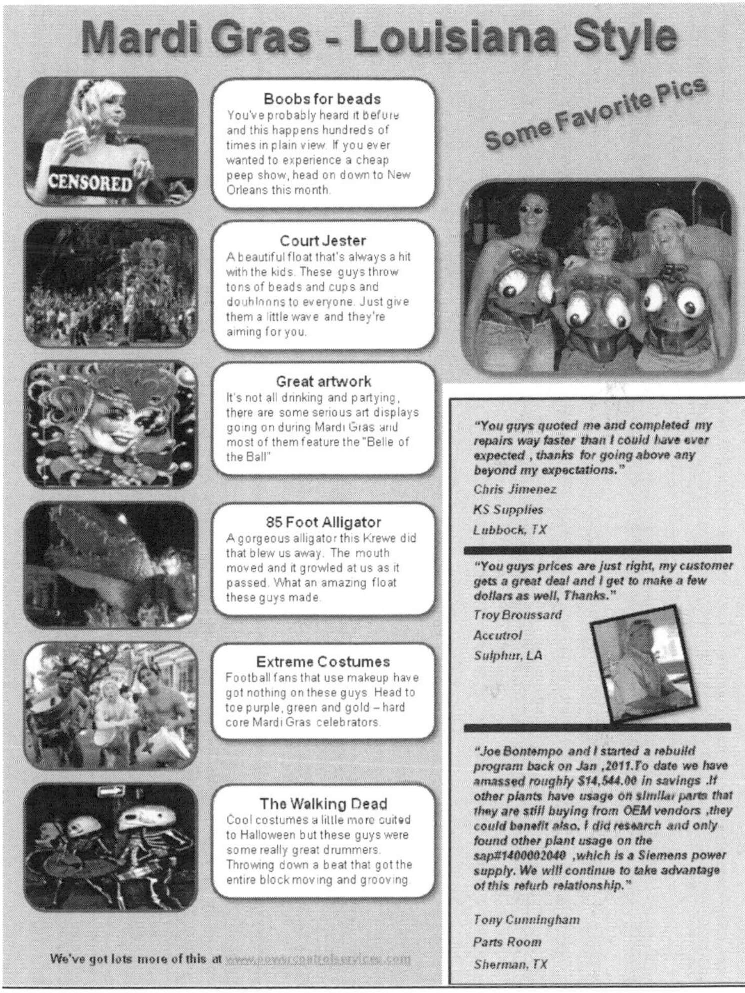

Mardi Gras - Louisiana Style

Some Favorite Pics

Boobs for beads
You've probably heard it before and this happens hundreds of times in plain view. If you ever wanted to experience a cheap peep show, head on down to New Orleans this month.

Court Jester
A beautiful float that's always a hit with the kids. These guys throw tons of beads and cups and doubloons to everyone. Just give them a little wave and they're aiming for you.

Great artwork
It's not all drinking and partying, there are some serious art displays going on during Mardi Gras and most of them feature the "Belle of the Ball"

85 Foot Alligator
A gorgeous alligator this Krewe did that blew us away. The mouth moved and it growled at us as it passed. What an amazing float these guys made.

Extreme Costumes
Football fans that use makeup have got nothing on these guys. Head to toe purple, green and gold – hard core Mardi Gras celebrators.

The Walking Dead
Cool costumes a little more suited to Halloween but these guys were some really great drummers. Throwing down a beat that got the entire block moving and grooving.

We've got lots more of this at [illegible]

"You guys quoted me and completed my repairs way faster than I could have ever expected , thanks for going above any beyond my expectations."

Chris Jimenez
KS Supplies
Lubbock, TX

"You guys prices are just right, my customer gets a great deal and I get to make a few dollars as well, Thanks."

Troy Broussard
Accutrol
Sulphur, LA

"Joe Bontempo and I started a rebuild program back on Jan ,2011.To date we have amassed roughly $14,544.00 in savings .If other plants have usage on similar parts that they are still buying from OEM vendors ,they could benefit also. I did research and only found other plant usage on the sap#1400002040 ,which is a Siemens power supply. We will continue to take advantage of this refurb relationship."

Tony Cunningham
Parts Room
Sherman, TX

I have many more examples and details of this at:
www.walterbergeron.com

Just Joking

Prejean and Boudreaux were fishing in the bayou when Prejean pulled out a cigar. Finding he had no matches, he asked Boudreaux for a light.'Yeah, ma fren, I haff a lighter,' Boudreaux replied with his thick Cajun accent, and then reaching into his tackle box, he pulled out a Bic lighter 10 inches long.'Holy shit, man!' exclaimed Prejean, taking the huge Bic lighter in his hands.'Where'd yew git dat monster?" Well,' replied Boudreaux, 'I got it from my Genie."You haff a Genie?' Prejean asked.'Yeah, ma fren. It's right here in my tackle box,' says Boudreaux.'Could I see him?'Boudreaux opens his tackle box and sure enough, out pops the Genie. Addressing the Genie, Prejean says, 'Hey dere! I'm a good buddy of your master. Will you grant me one wish?"Yes, I will,' says the Genie. So Prejean asked the Genie for a million bucks. The Genie disappears back into the tackle box leaving Prejean sitting there waiting for his million bucks.

Shortly, the Louisiana sky darkens and is filled with the sound of a million ducks....flying directly overhead. Over the roar of the million ducks Prejean yells at Boudreaux, 'What the hell? I asked for a million bucks, not a million ducks!'Boudreaux answers, 'Yeah, I forgot to tell yew, dat da Genie is hard of hearing. Do yew really tink I asked for a 10 inch Bic?'

A way to a woman's heart.. FLOWERS! .. psst.. real ones

Before us sits the infamous "Valentine's Day Killer."

Show'n You The Love
♥ Deal ♥

FREE RUSH UPGRADE!♥

♥ Ship us your equipment today

♥ Approve your quote in 3 days

♥ We fix it for you in 2 days

Show'n You Even More Love

FREE SHIPPING – to us and then back to you!

♥ just preapprove the quote before you ship it to us

Ship your equipment to:
Power Control Services
3827 Pinhook Road
Broussard, La. 70518
www.PowerControlServices.com

I have many more examples and details of this at:
www.walterbergeron.com

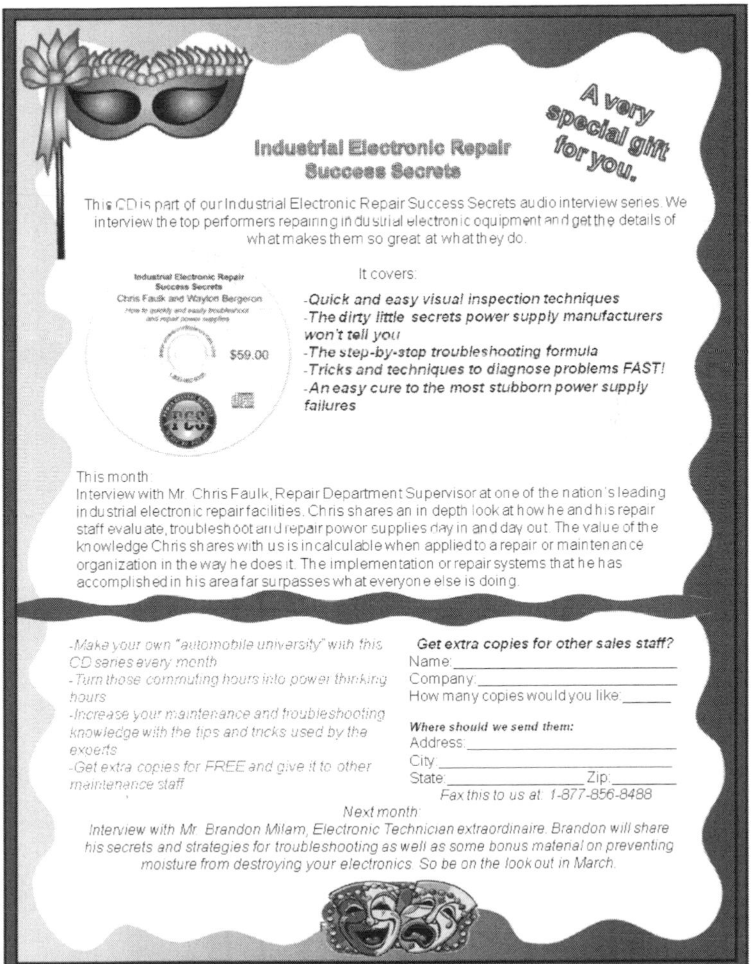

A very special gift for you.
Industrial Electronic Repair Success Secrets
This CD is part of our Industrial Electronic Repair Success Secrets audio interview series. We interview the top performers repairing industrial electronic equipment and get the details of what makes them so great at what they do.
Industrial Electronic Repair Success Secrets
Chris Faulk and Waylon Bergeron
$59.00
It covers:
-Quick and easy visual inspection techniques
-The dirty little secrets power supply manufacturers won't tell you
-The step-by-step troubleshooting formula
-Tricks and techniques to diagnose problems FAST!
-An easy cure to the most stubborn power supply failures
This month:
Interview with Mr. Chris Faulk, Repair Department Supervisor at one of the nation's leading industrial electronic repair facilities. Chris shares an in depth look at how he and his repair staff evaluate, troubleshoot and repair power supplies day in and day out. The value of the knowledge Chris shares with us is incalculable when applied to a repair or maintenance organization in the way he does it. The implementation or repair systems that he has accomplished in his area far surpasses what everyone else is doing.
-Make your own "automobile university" with this CD series every month
-Turn those commuting hours into power thinking hours
-Increase your maintenance and troubleshooting knowledge with the tips and tricks used by the experts
-Get extra copies for FREE and give it to other maintenance staff
Get extra copies for other sales staff?
Name:
Company:
How many copies would you like:
Where should we send them:
Address:
City:
State: Zip:
Fax this to us at: 1-877-856-8488
Next month:
Interview with Mr. Brandon Milam, Electronic Technician extraordinaire. Brandon will share his secrets and strategies for troubleshooting as well as some bonus material on preventing moisture from destroying your electronics. So be on the look out in March.

I have many more examples and details of this at:
www.walterbergeron.com

HAPPY ST. PATRICK'S DAY

Fix'n It

Newsletter

March 2012

INDUSTRIAL ELECTRONIC EQUIPMENT REPAIR SERVICES FOR DISTRIBUTORS

IN THIS ISSUE

Get it all online at:
www.powercontrolservices.com/Newsletter-March2012

Top 10 Stupid Facts About St. Patricks Day

1. The first St. Patrick's Day parade took place not in Ireland, but in the United States. Boston in 1737.
2. The phrase, "Drowning The Shamrock" is from the custom of floating the shamrock on the top of whiskey before drinking it. The Irish believe that if you keep the custom, then you will have a prosperous year.
3. In Chicago, on St. Patrick's Day, the rivers are dyed green. In New York, the rivers are green, but not by choice.
4. Legend has it, if you kiss the Blarney Stone, it is believed you will be given the "Gift of the Gab." Ever heard of Kathy Griffin? You get our point.
5. There are 34 million U.S. residents who claim Irish ancestry. This number is almost nine times the population of Ireland itself (3.9 million). Irish is the nation's second most frequently reported ancestry after German.
6. Surprisingly, St. Patrick's Day is supposed to be a religious holiday. Irish Catholics begin their day by attending mass and shops and businesses are closed to give everyone a day off to be spent with family and friends. We think barrels of sacrificial wine must be passed around at mass to keep these folks packing it in.
7. St. Patrick himself was not Irish, but English.
8. In the grounds of Downpatrick Cathedral, a large stone slab marks the grave of three saints, St. Colomb, St. Bridget and St. Patrick, who between them were responsible for converting the pagan Irish to Christianity. St. Patrick is the most famous of them all. In honor of his memory, the town of Downpatrick holds an annual parade, drawing more than 15,000 people.
9. Over 40% of the United States Presidents had Irish ancestors. At least 37% of US Presidents (16 out of 43) were alcoholics. Coincidence? I think not.
10. Irish legend has it you can track a leprechaun (a fairy resembling small shoe cobbler) by the sound of his hammer. Once you catch the bugger, threaten torture if he doesn't tell you where his treasure is. Unfortunately, robbing shoemakers is no longer accepted practice in the United States.

Never pay for another electronic failure again! Ever!

Now just imagine the look of shock and awe on your clients face when you tell him that! Imagine the disbelief he's going to experience when he realizes that he'll never have to find another vendor for repairs, because you'll now be able to service him for a lifetime. Well that's exactly what the **Platinum Level Rebuild Program** is all about and you are missing out. NOT being able to offer this to your clients is a grave error and you may be left out if you don't take action and enroll into the program right now while you still can.

But there's a catch!

We can't take everyone! Not even the luck of the Irish can help the fact that we only have room for 27 more distributors and then we are going to stop offering the enrollment so that we offer only the best level of service to those that are enrolled. We already have distributors in the following areas:

Albany, Georgia
Bedford, Ohio
Cedar Rapids, Iowa
Cleveland West, Ohio
Columbia, Missouri
Columbus, Ohio
Defiance, Ohio
Des Moines, Iowa
Erie, Pennsylvania
Fontana, California
Fort Wayne, Indiana
Fredericksburg, Virginia
Halton City, Texas
Jackson, Tennessee
Jonesboro, Arkansas
Kenosha, Wisconsin
Macon, Georgia
Memphis, Tennessee
Modesto, California
North Hollywood, California
Pasco, Washington
Scottsboro, Alabama
Sedalia, Missouri
St. Louis, Missouri
Texarkana, Texas
Tyler, Texas

Go to www.powercontrolservices.com/platinum right now to register for the next webinar to find out all of the amazing secrets behind this programs success!!!

I have many more examples and details of this at:
www.walterbergeron.com

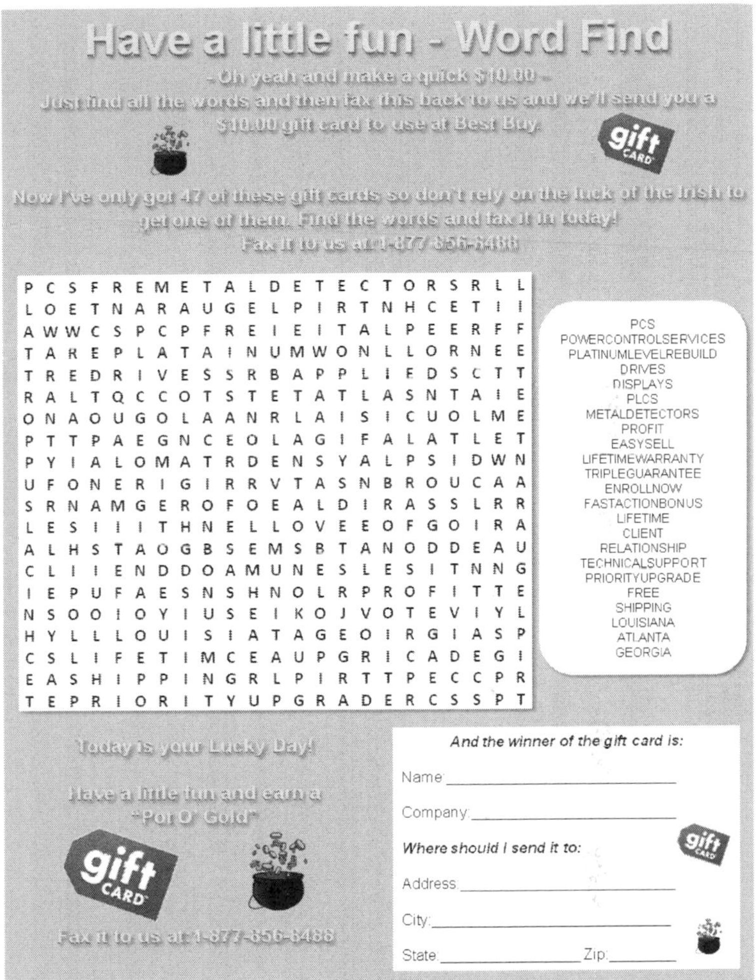

Have a little fun - Word Find

- Oh yeah and make a quick $10.00 -

Just find all the words and then fax this back to us and we'll send you a $10.00 gift card to use at Best Buy.

Now I've only got 47 of these gift cards so don't rely on the luck of the Irish to get one of them. Find the words and fax it in today!

Fax it to us at 1-877-856-6488

P	C	S	F	R	E	M	E	T	A	L	D	E	T	E	C	T	O	R	S	R	L	L
L	O	E	T	N	A	R	A	U	G	E	L	P	I	R	T	N	H	C	E	T	I	I
A	W	W	C	S	P	C	P	F	R	E	I	E	I	T	A	L	P	E	E	R	F	F
T	A	R	E	P	L	A	T	A	I	N	U	M	W	O	N	L	L	O	R	N	E	E
T	R	E	D	R	I	V	E	S	S	R	B	A	P	P	L	I	E	D	S	C	T	T
R	A	L	T	Q	C	C	O	T	S	T	E	T	A	T	L	A	S	N	T	A	I	E
O	N	A	O	U	G	O	L	A	A	N	R	L	A	I	S	I	C	U	O	L	M	E
P	T	T	P	A	E	G	N	C	E	O	L	A	G	I	F	A	L	A	T	L	E	T
P	Y	I	A	L	O	M	A	T	R	D	E	N	S	Y	A	L	P	S	I	D	W	N
U	F	O	N	E	R	I	G	I	R	R	V	T	A	S	N	B	R	O	U	C	A	A
S	R	N	A	M	G	E	R	O	F	O	E	A	L	D	I	R	A	S	S	L	R	R
L	E	S	I	I	I	T	H	N	E	L	L	O	V	E	E	O	F	G	O	I	R	A
A	L	H	S	T	A	O	G	B	S	E	M	S	B	T	A	N	O	D	D	E	A	U
C	L	I	I	E	N	D	D	O	A	M	U	N	E	S	L	E	S	I	T	N	N	G
I	E	P	U	F	A	E	S	N	S	H	N	O	L	R	P	R	O	F	I	T	T	E
N	S	O	O	I	O	Y	I	U	S	E	I	K	O	J	V	O	T	E	V	I	Y	L
H	Y	L	L	L	O	U	I	S	I	A	T	A	G	E	O	I	R	G	I	A	S	P
C	S	L	I	F	E	T	I	M	C	E	A	U	P	G	R	I	C	A	D	E	G	I
E	A	S	H	I	P	P	I	N	G	R	L	P	I	R	T	T	P	E	C	C	P	R
T	E	P	R	I	O	R	I	T	Y	U	P	G	R	A	D	E	R	C	S	S	P	T

PCS
POWERCONTROLSERVICES
PLATINUMLEVELREBUILD
DRIVES
DISPLAYS
PLCS
METALDETECTORS
PROFIT
EASYSELL
LIFETIMEWARRANTY
TRIPLEGUARANTEE
ENROLLNOW
FASTACTIONBONUS
LIFETIME
CLIENT
RELATIONSHIP
TECHNICALSUPPORT
PRIORITYUPGRADE
FREE
SHIPPING
LOUISIANA
ATLANTA
GEORGIA

Today is your Lucky Day!

Have a little fun and earn a "Pot O' Gold"

Fax it to us at 1-877-856-6488

And the winner of the gift card is:

Name: ____________________

Company: ____________________

Where should I send it to:

Address: ____________________

City: ____________________

State: ____________ Zip: ________

I have many more examples and details of this at:
www.walterbergeron.com

Two Irishmen move from Dublin to London to make their fortune. When they get there they decide to split living costs. Paddy pays the rent and Seamus buys the food.

The first day in their new flat Paddy comes home after work and says to Seamus "I paid the landlord. Did ye get the food Seamus. Seamus replies "Sure I did Paddy. Its in the fridge." Dats great " says Paddy, "Oim starvin" So he opens the fridge and there's about 50 bottles of Guiness in there. Then he sees at the bottom corner just half a loaf of stale bread.

"Are we having some kind of house warmin tonight" says Paddy. " No, sure we're not" says Seamus.

"Then what's all the bread for"

What do you get when you cross a pillowcase with a stone?
A sham rock

Two Irish friends greeted each other while waiting their turn at the bank window. "This reminds me of Finnegan," remarked one.

"What about Finnegan?" inquired the other.

"'Tis a story that Finnegan died, and when he greeted St. Peter, he said: 'It's a fine job you've had here for a long time.' 'Well, Finnegan,' said St. Peter, 'here we count a million years as a minute and a million dollars as a cent.' 'Ah!' said Finnegan, 'I'm needing cash. Lend me a cent.' 'Sure,' said St. Peter, 'just wait a minute.'"

Mrs. Feeney shouted from the kitchen, "Is that you I hear spittin' in the vase on the mantlepiece?" "No," said himself, "but I'm gettin' closer all the time!"

Brenda O'Malley is home making dinner as usual, when Tim Finnegan arrives at her door.
"Brenda, may I come in?" he asks. "I've somethin' to tell ya."
"Of course you can come in. You're always welcome, Tim. But where's my husband?"
"That's what I'm here to be tellin' ya, Brenda. There was an accident down at the Guinness brewery."
"Oh, God no!" cries Brenda. "Please don't tell me..."
"I must, Brenda. Your husband Shamus is dead and gone. I'm sorry."
Finally, she looked up at Tim. "How did it happen, Tim?"
"It was terrible, Brenda. He fell into a vat of Guinness and drowned."
"Oh my dear Jesus! But you must tell me true, Tim. Did he at least go quickly?"
"Well, no. Fact is, he got out three times to take a pee.

What's irish and stays out all night?
"Paddy O' Furniture"

O'Connell was staggering home with a pint of booze in his back pocket when he slipped and fell badly. Struggling to his feet, he felt something wet running down his leg.
"Please, God," he implored, "let it be blood!"

St. Patrick driving the snakes out of Ireland

How can you tell if an Irishman is having a good time?
He's Dublin over with laughter!

Please accept my most sincere apology

Last month I got caught up in the Mardi Gras spirit, maybe a little too caught up and put a picture in our "Just Joking" column that may have been offensive. I sincerely apologize if in my own personal excitement for Mardi Gras I offended you. Sorry.

I have many more examples and details of this at: www.walterbergeron.com

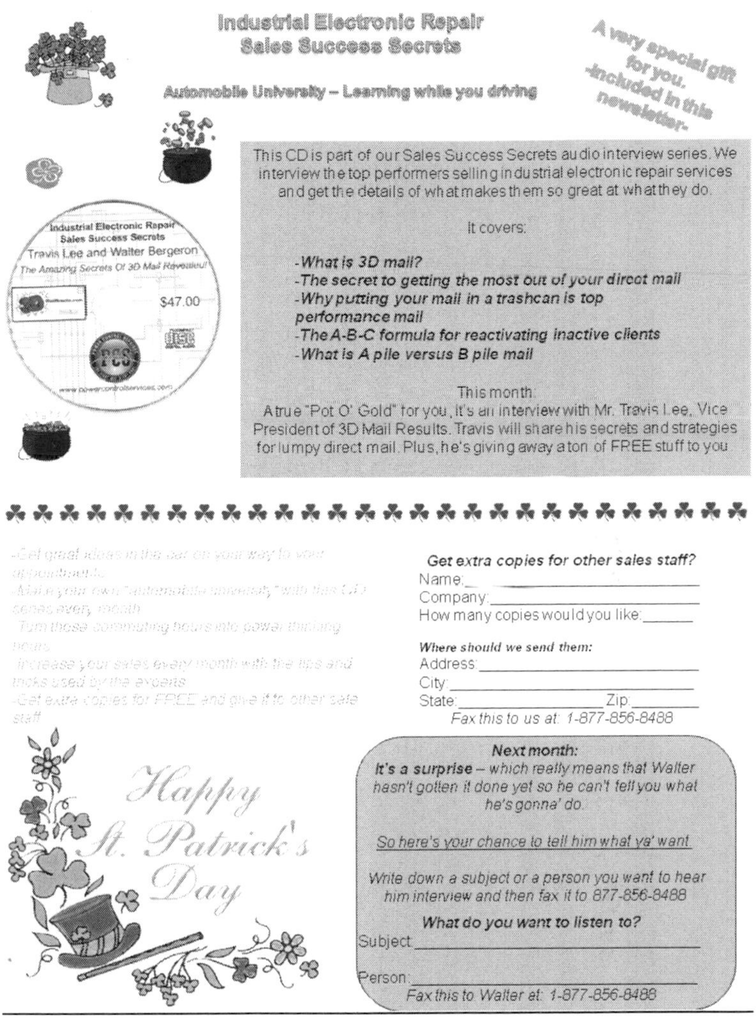

Industrial Electronic Repair
Sales Success Secrets

Automobile University – Learning while you driving

A very special gift for you. -Included in this newsletter-

Industrial Electronic Repair
Sales Success Secrets
Travis Lee and Walter Bergeron
The Amazing Secrets Of 3D Mail Revealed!
$47.00
www.powercontrolservices.com

This CD is part of our Sales Success Secrets audio interview series. We interview the top performers selling industrial electronic repair services and get the details of what makes them so great at what they do.

It covers:

- ***What is 3D mail?***
- ***The secret to getting the most out of your direct mail***
- ***Why putting your mail in a trashcan is top performance mail***
- ***The A-B-C formula for reactivating inactive clients***
- ***What is A pile versus B pile mail***

This month:
A true "Pot O' Gold" for you, it's an interview with Mr. Travis Lee, Vice President of 3D Mail Results. Travis will share his secrets and strategies for lumpy direct mail. Plus, he's giving away a ton of FREE stuff to you

-Get great ideas in the car on your way to your appointments
-Make your own "automobile university" with this CD series every month
-Turn those commuting hours into power thinking hours
-Increase your sales every month with the tips and tricks used by the experts
-Get extra copies for FREE and give it to other sale staff

Get extra copies for other sales staff?
Name:____________________
Company:____________________
How many copies would you like:______

Where should we send them:
Address:____________________
City:____________________
State:__________ Zip:________
Fax this to us at: 1-877-856-8488

Happy St. Patrick's Day

Next month:
It's a surprise *– which really means that Walter hasn't gotten it done yet so he can't tell you what he's gonna' do.*

So here's your chance to tell him what ya' want.

Write down a subject or a person you want to hear him interview and then fax it to 877-856-8488

What do you want to listen to?
Subject:____________________
Person:____________________
Fax this to Walter at: 1-877-856-8488

I have many more examples and details of this at:
www.walterbergeron.com

<u>Tyson Newsletter – Niche of 73 Tyson distributors</u>

Content:

Monthly reporting of Tyson activity and savings reports

Results:

No new clients or sales can be directly attributed to this newsletter

Cost Per Lead –$infinite per lead

Cost Per Sale – $infinite per sale currently

Electronic Repair Program

Tyson

Newsletter February 2012

INFORMATION NEEDED TO ACHIEVE THE MAXIMUM BENEFIT FROM THE TYSON REPAIR PROGRAM

IN THIS ISSUE

Get it all online at:
www.powercontrolservices.com/Tyson

Imposters are among us!!!

Be on the lookout for Power & Control Resources - Dyersburg, TN

- they are an imposter trying to weasel their way into this program -

They are not part of ANY program with Tyson or Applied Industrial Technologies

DO NOT USE THEM FOR REPAIRS!

THEY ARE NOT THE SAME AS PCS (Power Control Services) The ONLY place to send repairs for this program is to Atlanta, GA or Broussard, LA – otherwise Tyson will not get the savings they contracted as part of this program.

BEYOND ECONOMICAL REPAIR
End of the world?

You may have had a piece of equipment quoted to you as *Beyond Economical Repair* or *BER*, does this mean that you should use another facility for all your repairs?

– NONSENSE! –

All BER means is that piece of equipment is too badly damaged to be repaired reliably AND (*now here's the real kicker*) in good enough condition for a LONG TERM WARRANTY. Now there are going to be times when PCS may have BER'd a piece of equipment and someone else temporarily patched it together – that's a short term solution because you didn't get the long-term warranty you deserve.

Remember, the only place you'll ever get a lifetime warranty is with Power Control Services.

Success Story

Joe Bontempo and I started a rebuild program back on Jan ,2011. To date we have amassed roughly $14,544.00 in savings. If other plants have usage on similar parts that they are still buying from OEM vendors ,they could benefit also. I did research and only found other plant usage on the SAP#1400002040, which is a Siemens power supply. We will continue to take advantage of this repair relationship.

Tony Cunningham
Parts Room

THANK YOU

We would like to send a very special Thank you to the Applied Service Centers that participated in the Tyson program during the month of January 2012.

DeQueen, AR	*Macon, GA*
El Paso, TX	*North Sioux City, SD*
Fort Smith, AR	*Raleigh, NC*
Greenwood, SC	*Richland, MS*
Harrisonburg, VA	*Sedalia, MO*
Joplin, MO	*Springdale, AR*

Remember we've got that Tyson webpage that's got reports and videos and lots more information:
www.powercontrolservices.com/tyson
You can also get in touch with us directly at :
1-800-962-6355

APPLIED Industrial Technologies®

I have many more examples and details of this at: www.walterbergeron.com

January 2012– Tyson Plant Participation and Savings

MANUFACTURER	PART NUMBER	DESCRIPT	REPAIR AMOUNT	NEW COST
[illegible]	[illegible]	[illegible]	[illegible]	[illegible]

I have many more examples and details of this at:
www.walterbergeron.com

Platinum Program Newsletter – Niche of 231 Platinum Level eligible and enrolled distributors

Content:

Monthly reporting of Platinum Level Program members activity and new members

Results:

4 New Clients resulting in $14,429.37 in sales to date plus Lifetime Client Value of $138,303.80

Cost Per Lead –$129.94 per lead

Cost Per Sale – $15.75 per sale currently and will go to $.21 over lifetime of client

Platinum Level Rebuild Program

Newsletter

December 2011

INFORMATION NEEDED TO ACHIEVE THE MAXIMUM BENEFIT FROM THIS PROGRAM

Welcome to the first newsletter specifically for the Platinum Level Rebuild Program.

In it we will make sure we keep all Applied Service Center's and associated personnel up to date on the monthly happenings with the program, as well as some things that have absolutely nothing to do with this to keep it more interesting. If you want to make sure someone else gets a copy of this on a monthly basis or if you want to stop getting these, please feel free to email us at info@powercontrolservices.com and we'll help you out right away.

Enjoy

It's not a rumor – we really are repairing Safeline Metal Detectors and giving them a Lifetime Warranty

A warranty that never runs out, we will repair the control module and/or power supply forever for FREE and ConAgra/Nestle will never, ever have to pay for another repair on it again – ever!

Get a look at the "drowning the circuit board in the pool" video

Full details at:

www.powercontrolservices.com/safeline

You can also get in touch with us directly at :

1-800-962-6355

Christmas decorations during football?!?!

I just spent the entire weekend engulfed in Christmas decorations. A weekend when the Saints are fixing to go 9-3 and LSU is 13-0. My wife is a bit of a decorating nut, but do we really have to do it all THIS weekend? We already start decorating for Halloween in late August, Thanksgiving decorations go up November 1st, rain or shine, and Christmas gets going just as soon as I finish my last piece of Turkey on Thanksgiving Day. We got started Friday as I pulled in the driveway after work. Taking down lights, wreaths, ornaments, fake trees, bells, boxes, wrapping paper, and what seemed like 4 tons of stuff down my rickety little ladder going down from my attic. Then the real fun began. I was so very happy to check for burned out Christmas light bulbs for 3 hours, then wind up just throwing the *%$!@@# things away out of horrible frustration and buy the brand new million dollar a piece LED lights. I am sure I'll be replacing those next year.

And shoot me an email if you enjoy the sight of about 4732 feet of green extension cords strewn over the lawn to light up Santa, reindeer, trees, light strings (new LED ones) and lots of miscellaneous elves, etc.. Oh yeah, don't forget to put on your safety harness cause you're going up on that 70% grade roof in the rain to hang a few strands of lights there too. This rant doesn't even cover the inside decorations, that's the rest of the weekend in between the Saints game and LSU (I draw the line in the sand at missing BOTH games) actually I got to decorate the tree during half time – My wife is so understanding. I am really not a scrooge, Christmas is sincerely one of my favorite times of the year, I am just glad decorations are out of the way so now I can enjoy some egg nog and couch time.

THANK YOU

We would like to send a very special Thank You to the Applied Service Centers that achieved the highest level of participation in the Platinum Level Rebuild program during the month of November 2011.

Pasco, WA

A very special Thank You Chris La Plante and the entire staff at the Pasco Service Center, it's takes a team effort to get those P.O.'s approved. Chris and the staff were able to make well over $2000.00 on just one P.O. with the Platinum Level Rebuild Program – way to go guys!!

"Finally we have a po! On RMA SQ-132316, I am making up the order right now."

Chris La Plante
CSSR Supervisor

Remember we've got that Platinum webpage that's got reports and videos and lots more information:

www.powercontrolservices.com/platinum

You can also get in touch with us directly at :

1-800-962-6355

APPLIED Industrial Technologies®

I have many more examples and details of this at:
www.walterbergeron.com

A special appreciation goes out to all those Service Centers that are enrolled in the Platinum Level Rebuild Program

Albany, Georgia
Bedford, Ohio
Cedar Rapids, Iowa
Cleveland West, Ohio
Columbia, Missouri
Columbus, Ohio
Dos Moines, Iowa
Erie, Pennsylvania
Fontana, California
Fort Wayne, Indiana
Fredericksburg, Virginia
Haltom City, Texas
Kenosha, Wisconsin
Macon, Georgia
Memphis, Tennessee
Modesto, California
North Hollywood, California
Pasco, Washington
Scottsboro, Alabama
St Louis, Missouri
Tyler, Texas

This is everyone that filled out the enrollment form and we received it – If your Service Center is not listed, go to www.powercontrolservices.com/platinum or call us immediately at 1-800-962-6355 and we'll get that enrollment form over to you right away. Don't wait – do it now before we fill up enrollment in the program.

Top Questions of the Month

Question:
Why is Christmas like any other day at the office?
Answer:
You end up doing all the work and the fat guy in the suit gets all the credit.

Question:
I already have some equipment at the repair center for ConAgra or Nestle. Will you give me an RMA for that equipment?
Answer:
Of course, we want to get as much equipment quoted as we can so we will certainly re-quote you on equipment we already have for ConAgra or Nestle, just let call us at 1-800-962-6355 and we'll get that right over to you.

Question:
What happens if you don't have a price for a piece of equipment?
Answer:
We'll send you an RMA anyway so you can send it to us with Free shipping, the price will be zero until we can get you an accurate quote upon evaluation.

Question:
It was Christmas Eve in a supermarket and a woman was anxiously picking over the last few remaining turkeys, looking for a really large one. In desperation she called over an assistant and asked "Excuse me, do these turkeys get any bigger?"
Answer:
"No" he replied, "They're all dead".

Question:
ConAgra/Nestle say the price is too high, they can get it repaired somewhere else for cheaper?

Answer:
Repaired for cheaper – yes, they might be able to, but not rebuilt and never have to ever pay for another repair again. Make sure you let them know just what an extraordinary value this is to them.

You see, the average repair will last about 1 year, but for the sake of argument we'll say their repairs are twice as good as the average repair and it will last them for 2 years. And let's say they keep their equipment only 10 years before they completely upgrade the entire system with new equipment, most manufacturers wait at least 15 years, but this is worst case so we'll say 10. And we'll say our price is $300 and the normal repair cost is only $100.

So if they get their equipment repaired once every 2 years for 10 years, that's 5 repairs at a cost of $500, but with the Platinum Level Rebuild Program they would only pay $300 and that still does not take into account that they don't pay shipping or that the equipment will last longer since this is a complete rebuild and not just a patch type repair.

This program is so much less expensive and has a tremendously higher reliability than a standard repair – ConAgra and Nestle are flushing money away by not taking advantage of this program at every opportunity.

I have many more examples and details of this at:
www.walterbergeron.com

Platinum Level Rebuild Program

Newsletter

February 2012

INFORMATION NEEDED TO ACHIEVE THE MAXIMUM BENEFIT FROM THIS PROGRAM

IN THIS ISSUE

Get it all online at:
www.powercontrolservices.com/Platinum

Mardi Gras - Louisiana Style

85 Foot Alligator
A gorgeous alligator this Krewe did that blew us away. The mouth moved and it growled at us as it passed. What an amazing float these guys made.

Really Terrible Valentines Day Jokes

Q: What do squirrels give for Valentine's Day?
A: Forget-me-nuts.
Q: What did the valentine card say to the stamp?
A: Stick with me and we'll go places!
Q: What did the light bulb say to the switch?
A: You turn me on.
Q: Did Adam and Eve ever have a date?
A: No, but they had an Apple.
Q: What did the boy octopus say to the girl octopus?
A: Can I hold your hand, hand, hand, hand, hand, hand, hand, hand, hand?
Q: What did one snake say to the other snake?
A: Give me a little hug and a hiss, honey.
Q: Why did the banana go out with the prune?
A: Because it couldn't get a date.
Q: What is a ram's favorite song on February 14th?
A: I only have eyes for ewe, dear
Q: What travels around the world but stays in one corner?
A: A stamp.
Q: What happens when you fall in love with a French chef?
A: You get buttered up.
Q: What is a vampire's sweetheart called?
A: His ghoul-friend.
Q: If your aunt ran off to get married, what would you call her?
A: Antelope.

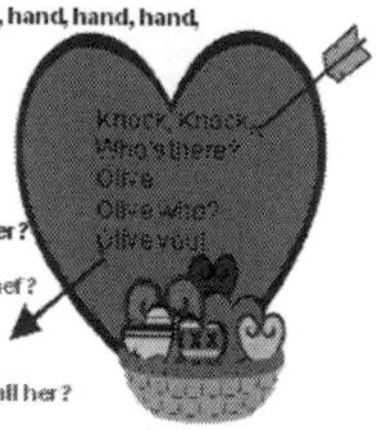

Mardi Gras or Fat Tuesday or Carnival
February 21st, 2012

Imposters are among us!!!

STOP

Be on the lookout for Power & Control Resources - Dyersburg, TN

- they are an imposter trying to weasel their way into this program -

They are not part of ANY program with ConAgra or Nestle or any national account with Applied Industrial Technologies

DO NOT USE THEM FOR REPAIRS!

THEY ARE NOT THE SAME AS PCS (Power Control Services)
The ONLY place to send repairs for this program is to Atlanta, GA or Broussard, LA – otherwise you will not get the savings that are contracted as part of this program.

The list on the back page includes all enrolled service centers. If your name is not there then go to:
www.powercontrolservices.com/Platinum
And get registered for the enrollment webinar

APPLIED
Industrial Technologies®

I have many more examples and details of this at:
www.walterbergeron.com

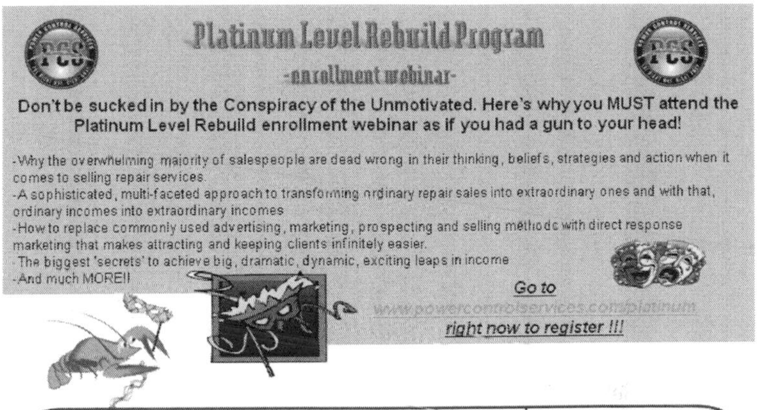

Platinum Level Rebuild Program
-enrollment webinar-
Don't be sucked in by the Conspiracy of the Unmotivated. Here's why you MUST attend the Platinum Level Rebuild enrollment webinar as if you had a gun to your head!
-Why the overwhelming majority of salespeople are dead wrong in their thinking, beliefs, strategies and action when it comes to selling repair services.
-A sophisticated, multi-faceted approach to transforming ordinary repair sales into extraordinary ones and with that, ordinary incomes into extraordinary incomes
-How to replace commonly used advertising, marketing, prospecting and selling methods with direct response marketing that makes attracting and keeping clients infinitely easier.
-The biggest 'secrets' to achieve big, dramatic, dynamic, exciting leaps in income
-And much MORE!!
Go to
www.powercontrolservices.com/platinum
right now to register !!!

I have many more examples and details of this at:
www.walterbergeron.com

Platinum Level Rebuild Campaign – Distributor Clients

Content:

Standard Catalog

-CD in a CD holder attached to cover of catalog

-Customizable Tri-fold brochure – this was a way for our sales staff to allow distributor clients to put their logo on a marketing piece we created for them.

-Business card in a holder – the back of the business card contains an offer for client to direct respond

-Exterior Folder is a step by step process for sales person to use to walk client through our sales process

Video Case with Platinum Level Rebuild webinar installed

Results:

We considered this outrageous because of the sheer size of it – size DOES matter and the uniqueness of the cover as an all in one package for ease of use for our outside sales staff as well as Video Case make this campaign just as effective as an in person salesman visiting them.

2011 – New distributors using this item - 10 resulting in $33,486.45 in actual sales in 2011 with a Lifetime Client Value of $345,759.50

Cost Per Lead –$495.16 per lead

Cost Per Sale – $110.94 per sale currently and will go to $2.45 over lifetime of client

<u>Gold Level repair Program – End User Clients.</u>

Content:

Mega credibility catalog with step by step instructions on what actions to take next and top requested questions answered on the cover.

Results:

We considered this outrageous because of the sheer size of it – size DOES matter and the way we step our clients directly through our sales process in order to take advantage of our services as well as it answers the most frequently asked questions

2011 – New end users - 18 resulting in $4,397.43 in actual 2011 sales with a Lifetime Client Value of $69,884.46

Cost Per Lead –$193.32 per lead

Cost Per Sale – $414.25 per sale currently and will go to $26.08 over lifetime of client

Chapter Six

Getting Past My Personal Barriers With Coaching

It was early in December as we began planning our Christmas gift list for family and friends and my wife had just spoken with me in detail about her desires for Christmas morning. Now she and I are usually pretty practical most of the time and usually we ask for things we need or things that we are going to get anyway, but to make it easy on each other we let the other person get it for us. So she gave me a few practical items and I heard in our conversations over the past few months something she wanted that I was going to add to her list. Something that would excite and surprise her. Then it was my turn to tell her what I wanted for Christmas.

I had been rehearsing this for a few days, I knew exactly what I was going to ask for and the caveat that might make it a NO WAY answer to my request. So in my mind over the past few days I had said to myself "I would like to attend Lee Milteer's Implementation Group and I especially want you to join the group with me". So over and over I rehearsed this in my mind to make sure it had some impact and that she knew I was serious and sincere about this request. Now here we were and it was my turn to speak and what I said was "I want Lee Milteer to implement with you and me" …

Now it was a bit late in the evening and I could see by the lines on her forehead that I said something wrong. Jana was aware who Lee Milteer was and had seen a few photos of this beautiful long haired blonde model of a woman on a few books that I had been reading and marketing pieces from GKIC. She was not too happy that I was bringing another woman's name into our conversation, especially a blonde woman that looked like Lee does, so her response was "You want Lee to implement with you and me?"

Did you ever have an out of body experience or truly wish you could get a mulligan or a do-over in life, well this was one of those moments for me. For the next 30 minutes I stumbled many times re-asking the question and clarifying what I meant by implement and the role of another woman in this. After many apologies and quite a bit of backtracking and reiterating my feelings for my wife, she agreed. WHEW! Not one of the smoothest moments of my life. So now Jana was on board with this, though I knew it was a reluctant agreement on her part and that she was not nearly as excited about this as I was. We are both committed in our marriage to support one another and this is just one of those things that loving spouses do for each other.

The promise made by this coaching group and I assumed by Lee Milteer herself was that she was going to double our business guaranteed. Now that's a pretty bold statement and an even bolder guarantee, especially to a business owner and entrepreneur. I was pretty confident that I was making the right moves for my business and growing it as fast as I comfortably could. For someone to tell me they could guarantee that my business would double in the next 24 months was something I couldn't pass up and I truly believed she could do it.

So in January of 2012 in Phoenix Arizona we had our first meeting with Lee Milteer and the Peak Performers Implementation Coaching Group. I had expectations from Lee that she would help us dig into the tactical business issues that we needed help with at that time. A few weeks before the meeting she instructed us to write a brief introduction of ourselves as well as 3 key issues in our business that we needed the group to help us with.

On the morning of the second day of this Implementation Coaching group Lee asked a very important question to all of us. She asked us if we were getting what we expected from this meeting? As I looked around the room, everyone was nodding their head in agreement and telling Lee yes that this is what they expected. I on the other hand decided I was going to tell Lee the truth about my experience and so very reluctantly I raised my hand and shook my head NO. Jana began to kick me under the table and nudge me in the side with her elbow to lower my hand before Lee could see what I was doing, but it was too late. It was at that moment that the clocks on the wall stopped, time stood still and silence filled the room as Lee stopped what she was doing and walked over to my table, pointed to me and asked me "What was it you were expecting?" I very humbly told Lee "Lee I was expecting a seminar, a lecture type atmosphere and then a round table type mastermind to work on my business and that is not at all what I got. What you did was go so much more in depth than that. You went to the heart of the roadblocks that were holding me back, not simply a tactical approach to a few business issues but a more root cause approach to my life, to step outside of my comfort zone and then on top of that you gave me knowledge and skills to immediately get past them."

Everything I said was true, Lee really did go so much deeper than I expected and it was because of that meeting that I decided to take even more action with my marketing. I recognized this as a pivotal point in my own personal and professional growth, sitting here with my wife and owning my ability to design a path for our lives was a choice that required action. A few days later I decided that I was going to apply for GKIC Marketer of the Year even though I had only been implementing their teachings for 90 days. I decided to go for it and see if I could at least get selected as a finalist.

I spent the next week gathering my marketing pieces together and tossing out the crap and keeping only the best stuff I had implemented and had results on. I prepared a video presentation explaining in a little detail what I had accomplished as well as including the overall results. This process forced me to organize my marketing system to a level of great detail as well as to continue to come up with new ways to have a bigger impact with my clients. I then followed the instructions for the submission and everything was printed out as well as on a CD. Then I put it all into our new video shock and awe box and threw in a HUGE Mardi Gras king cake and shipped it all to the Chicago GKIC offices.

Two days later I got a call from Ron Penksa with GKIC and said "Do you think you can bribe us with cake? Do you think all it takes is to butter us up with a little food and that we are going to let you into this exclusive club as a Marketer of the Year finalist?" He let me know I was playing with the big dogs and my competition was fierce, but he also let me know, just from the fact that he took the time to call, that my submission had one heck of an impact of the staff. Now all I could do was sit and wait for a response!

A week later or so Ron called me again and said that he just got finished with speaking to Bette T and Dave Dee and that they had just experienced my submission package for Marketer of the Year and that they thought I would be a prime candidate for **Dan Kennedy's Platinum Mastermind** group. Ron said that a spot had just opened up and that if I decided to join that I would have to write one really big check as well as be in Cleveland in 3 days to make the first meeting. Now there are times in your life when you need to make bold moves and take a leap of faith. Up to this point I thought I had been doing just that for the last few months with GKIC and as far as I was concerned I had written quite a few big checks to GKIC, but none as big as this. No move as bold as this one. Lee Milteer told me I needed to step outside my comfort zone and this decision was extremely outside of my comfort zone. After mulling it over for a few hours and spending some heart to heart time talking with Jana, we had decided we could afford to do it and that we would likely not get another opportunity like this ever, so we went for it!

3 Days later I was in Cleveland in a room with 20 other very successful entrepreneurs. I was sitting in a very tall chair with a microphone in my hand staring into the piercing eyes of some motivated and extremely intelligent business owners and entrepreneurs. Dan Kennedy is 2 feet away from me grilling me with detailed and probing questions about my business and he doesn't pull any punches. Dan Kennedy expects immediate and accurate answers. If you ever want to feel pressure, I suggest you experience a mastermind hot seat with Dan Kennedy, it'll be something you never forget.

Chapter Seven

Made It To The Short List

On March 26th I received a very inconspicuous and dull looking email from GKIC. It read something like "Hey Walter we would like to inform you that you have been selected as a finalist for the GKIC Marketer of the Year Blah, blah, blah and you need to do a 25 minute presentation at super conference in April."

OH YEAH BABY! I JUST MADE IT AS A FINALIST! I can't believe it, out of all the submissions and as little of a time as I have actually done what GKIC had been telling me to do, they selected me as a Top 7 Finalist. I called my contact at GKIC Ron Penksa and verified this was true and after a few moments of disbelief I settled into the fact that I had done it, but that this was just the beginning of a lot more work. Ron told me that competition was fierce and that I really needed to bring my "A" game to the super conference. If I had any chance of winning I had to take my presentation to a whole new level and win over the 1200 plus people as well as a panel of judges. The excitement was over and it was time to get to work on a killer presentation. So that's what I did.

Lee Milteer said something to me that I had heard a bazillion times before and I am sure I'll hear it again. She told me to visualize the outcome as I prepared for it. She explained that the mind can help make things happen if you can see it clearly enough and then take action on it. So, the next few weeks were filled with making a presentation that highlighted the most successful parts of my marketing system. Building stories around what I had accomplished as well as rehearsing timing and impact of the presentation so that it wouldn't be boring.

I also had to get my numbers accurate so that I could impress a panel of judges and be ready for some tough questions from 3 people that had accomplished way more than I had. I did all of this with the presumption that I would be selected as the winner and I prepared with just that attitude. I made up some 1 million dollar bills with a new website so I could prepare for the questions the crowd would have and give them a place to get copies of what I had prepared. I made some badge holders to give away to people I networked with at the super conference.

I emailed Lee Milteer letting her know that one of her coaching group members had been selected as a finalist and I asked her if I could give her a testimonial for the Peak Performers Implementation Coaching group. Now Lee has told us that you have to give in order to receive, so I offered her a testimonial and she gave me an opportunity. She asked me if I could prepare a 60 second testimonial and come up on stage with her at Superconference and give my testimonial to everyone. Did Lee Milteer just ask me to go up on stage with her? Did I just get an amazing opportunity to speak in front of 1200 of my peers? Yes I did and it was because I stepped outside of my comfort zone and offered something to someone else. Thank you Lee.

Chapter Eight

The Big Win

So away I went to Dallas Texas just days away from making a couple of presentations in front of 1200 people. As I attended the amazing seminars and listened to the spectacular speakers and absorbed this tremendous information I was completely confident that this would be a life changing event.

I got to meet Lee Milteer again and have a few private moments with her, she reassured me of her confidence in me and gave me a few tips on how to present myself and visualize winning the award. I was able to share the stage with Lee for a moment or two and share my testimonial for Peak Performers Implementation Coaching group and what it helped me to accomplish.

Bonus Day came a lot faster than I expected, but I was prepared and had gone over my presentation many, many times over the last few weeks. The morning came and I was to be the 5th presenter and I would go on around 2pm. So I sat and listened intently as the other finalists gave their presentations. My heart sank multiple times as the other finalists gave some truly amazing results and inspirational presentations, the competition was fierce and some of these guys truly nailed their performance and results. At one point I thought I might vote for someone else, they were that good!

2pm came and it was my turn up on stage. I brought my best performance to the audience and they responded with not just one, but two standing ovations! After I finished my presentation I turned to the judges and answered their many questions and then I was sent on my way.

Following my presentation, the audience had a 20 minute break. I was pretty sure I nailed it and then I was reassured of that when I got mobbed by the audience. I almost made it to the first aisle on my way back to my seat before the first mob hit me. They had cameras and cell phones grilling me with questions about my video case. I had to demonstrate how it worked and what the marketing campaign consisted of that led up to me sending such a shock and awe package out. They wanted to know how I qualified someone before I spent so much money on trying to convert this lead. 20 minutes later after Dave Dee told everyone to leave me alone and take their seats I finally got to sit down. The next two finalists completed their presentations and I did my best to focus on them but I honestly didn't hear much. My mind was racing as the adrenaline coursed through my body and slowly I calmed down, but I was still very happy with what I had managed to pull off.

A few minutes after the voting was completed they called all the finalists over to the corner of the massive convention center and told us the judges were deadlocked and that instead of one winner there were going to be two. They asked the seven of us if it would be OK if the two winners would split the prize money and we all agreed. They called us all on stage and our hearts were racing as Dave Dee announced the four top winners that would all be attending winners weekend with Dan Kennedy in Florida in January. Then Dave called out the third place winner "Donna Galante", applied her miraculous marketing to her practice in an impressive list of accomplishments as well as being invited to speak at the next GKIC women's event by Bette T. Next Dave announced the second place winner "John Rinaldi" who had a spectacular presentation of what an industrial marketer can do in an industry with little to no thought placed into direct marketing. Then Dave said "Congratulations to Walter Bergeron and Rick Schaeffer as winners of the GKIC Marketer of the Year" and then lots of applause and pictures and even a video interview from the stage. Holy cow what a ride!

My first phone call was to Jana to let her know the results, she had been texting me throughout the entire event but with all that I was required to do I wasn't able to get her minute by minute details so I made sure she was the first call I made.

And now, keep on implementing!

Walter Bergeron

Marketer of the Year

Here I am at my desk with the "Big Check" and all of the awards, enjoying a celebratory "Money Cookie" from the CEO of GKIC